Henry Tamburin

on

Casino Gambling

The Best of The Best

2ND EDITION

Research Services Unlimited

Casino Gambling Book Publishers

P.O.Box 19727 ▪ Greensboro, NC 27419

http://www.smartgaming.com

Address all inquiries to the publisher:
Research Services Unlimited, P.O. Box 19727, Greensboro, NC 27419

Manufactured in the United States of America

Cover design by Ben Jordan
Typeset by Michelle L. Canter-Ball

Second Edition, April 1998
ISBN: 0-912177-13-6
Library of Congress Catalog Card Number: 97-76199

Publisher's Cataloging-in-Publication
(Prepared by Quality Books, Inc.)

Tamburin, Henry J., 1944-
    Henry Tamburin on casino gambling : the best of the best
/ by Henry J. Tamburin. -- 2nd ed.
    p. cm.
    Includes bibliographical references and index.
    ISBN: 0-912177-13-6

    1. Gambling. 2. Gambling systems.   I. Title. II.
Title: Casino Gambling

GV1301.T36 1998   795
                           QBI97-41620

This book is dedicated to the memory of my friend and colleague, Dick Ramm, who was a brilliant gaming mathematician. His friendship and advice will be greatly missed.

ACKNOWLEDGEMENT

Thanks to all the editors from these publications with whom I worked.

Ante Up	Gambling Times*
Atlantic City Magazine	Gaming South
Bingo Bugle	Gaming Today
Boardwalker*	Jackpot (Gulfport)
Casino Player	Jackpot (New Mexico)
Casino Magazine*	Midwest Gaming & Travel
Chance & Circumstance	Mobile Press Register Newspaper
Crapshooter	The Experts Blackjack Newsletter*
Crapsmen Newsletter*	Times Observer Newspaper
Florida Player*	Win Magazine*

*no longer in print

Michelle L. Canter-Ball deserves my thanks for typesetting this book, Ben Jordan for another superb job in designing the cover, Etta Stuckey for her editorial assistance, and my wife, Linda, for putting it all together and publishing it.

I must also give thanks to my fellow gaming writers for the wisdom and knowledge I've gained in their published studies, newsletters, books, articles, and cyberspace chat groups and message boards. Thanks, guys, for making me a better player.

And last, but not least, I acknowledge my devoted readers for their kind words and letters expressing "thanks" for helping them become winners. You've made it all worthwhile.

TABLE OF CONTENTS

PREFACE

It was the summer of 1979. My heart was pounding with excitement as I thumbed through my copy of *Gambling Times* magazine that had just arrived with the mail. I finally found what I was searching for on page 16. It was the article *How's Your Gambling IQ?* A smile came to my face. It was my first published article on casino gambling.

In 1981, I did something unheard of. I convinced the editor of our local newspaper to let me write a weekly column on casino gambling that would benefit players. This was the birth of one of the first weekly newspaper columns of its kind, *Inside Gambling*, devoted solely to explaining how casino players can improve their odds.

These were the humble beginnings of my career as a casino gambling writer. From that point on, there was no stopping. The requests kept coming and I kept writing.

Now it's 1998 and at last count, I've written over 500 articles for 20 different publications and the book you are reading is my tenth. Along the way, I've been a guest speaker at hundreds of seminars, operated a gaming school for players, appeared on TV and radio, hosted my own web site, and been featured in three instructional gaming videos. Yes, I've come a long way from that first article in 1979.

Although I enjoy writing, I am first and foremost a player. After perfecting my blackjack card counting skills some 27 years ago, I've enjoyed beating the casinos at their own game. I also enjoy playing the other casino games but admit I do not spend a lot of time and money betting on games with a negative expectation; however, many players do. The advice in my articles and in this book will help the skilled and recreational player win more (and maybe lose less) while confidently playing his favorite game.

The idea for this book came from readers of my articles who would call or write and ask for copies. "Why not publish a book of your articles?" asked my wife. "Why not?" I thought.

The toughest part of creating this book was deciding which articles to include. I used feedback from readers, editors, friends, and business associates to select the articles they thought were some of my "best".

The organization of the articles was a no-brainer. I placed all the blackjack related articles together in one chapter, craps in another and so on. A complete listing of the articles in this book appears in the Table of Contents.

I made a decision early on to use the original articles that I submitted to editors rather than the edited version that appeared in print. This was more for convenience since most were in my computer files and the edited versions were not.

Some of the articles were written for regional publications in Atlantic City, Mississippi, or Las Vegas. Therefore, you will find reference to specific playing conditions or rules for those gaming jurisdictions. For the most part the theme of the article would be appropriate for other gaming localities as well.

Where I felt that an article needed to be updated, I included a note following the article. One thing I did change was the grammatical use of he/she or they when referring to players or dealers. After re-reading my articles I realized I wasn't consistent in this usage. So I decided on the generic "he" even though I am fully aware that at least 50% of the players and dealers are women.

I hope you enjoy reading my book on casino gambling and that it makes your gaming experience more fun and profitable. Feel free to e-mail your comments about the book directly to me at HTamburin@aol.com. Good luck and play smart!

Henry J. Tamburin

1

Basics of Casino Gambling

Understanding How Casinos Win

It's important you understand how casinos win as much as they do from players. After all, casinos don't charge admission and they certainly don't depend upon the luck of their dealers to generate the income they need to stay in business. In fact, they guarantee themselves a steady income by having a built-in advantage or house edge on every bet. The higher the casino's edge, the less is your chance of winning.

Let's look at two scenarios that occur when you gamble. You either win a bet or lose a bet. When you lose a bet, your bet is lost, period. End of discussion. But when you win a bet, you have a silent partner that shares in your good fortune - the casino! Here is how it works.

Instead of receiving a fair payout for winning a bet, the casino always pays you less. For example, a fair payout on a winning $1 bet on any single number in roulette is $37 since your odds of winning the bet to begin with are 37 to 1. When you win, the casino only pays you $35. It keeps the $2, like a tax (some partner!). The $2 sort of disappears into the casino's coffer without your even knowing about it.

What you need to know as a smart player is the amount

(or percent) of this hidden tax on every bet you plan to make and what you can do, if anything, to lower it. Remember that the lower you can reduce the casino's edge, the greater will be your chances of winning more or at least minimizing your losses.

Generally, the table games of blackjack, craps and baccarat offer the opportunity to make bets with a low casino edge. But you must learn specific playing strategies and focus on certain bets over others to take advantage of the lower edge. Some video poker and slot machines also offer a good deal to the player. It is possible, in fact, to turn the tables on the casino and actually have the advantage over them. Professional blackjack and video poker players do it day in and day out.

The bottom line is that smart casino players learn playing and betting strategies so that they never make a bet in a casino where the casino's edge is greater than 1.5%. By doing so, they will increase their chances of winning something or in the worst case, minimize their losses. It's the smart way to play.

◆ ◆ ◆

Don't Get Psyched Into Losing

Casinos have several advantages over players to generate the income they need to stay in business. The one that is the most obvious and well publicized is the mathematical advantage casinos have in all games (except a few played skillfully). They get their edge by simply not paying off winning bets at true odds. Anthony Curtis, publisher of the *Las Vegas Advisor*, gave one of the best layman definitions of the casino advantage when he stated: "casino gambling is a form of entertainment and *the casino advantage is the price of admission*".

Of course casino players have control over how much

"admission" they allow the casinos to charge them. Some casino games and some bets have a higher casino advantage than others. It behooves players, therefore, to cut the cost of admission to as low as possible by making only bets having the lowest casino advantage.

Is this all that is required to become a successful casino player? In my book, no. The other not-so-obvious casino advantage is the one engineered by the casinos to "psyche" players into losing.

Since casinos have the mathematical edge over most players, they know that as long as they can keep the players making bets on *their* tables or putting coins into *their* slot machines, they will ultimately win money and players will conversely lose money. The trick is to do this in a subtle way so that players do not feel bad about losing and will return again to potentially lose more. Remember that casinos live or die on their ability to attract repeat customers!

The 24-hour, non-stop party atmosphere in casinos is designed to make it easy for players to part with their money. Think about it. In a casino, the player is king and will be treated like royalty. You can indulge in just about anything. The casino environment screams for the player to let go of his inhibitions and "have a ball". As Marvin Karlins aptly put it in his classic book, *Psyching Out Vegas,* "there is no room for party-poopers in the manufactured gaiety of the casinos. Winners are heralded by the ringing of bells and the shouts of the dealers....this is a world where everything goes, it's fast, it's fun and it's loose so visitors 'let it all hang out'. Unfortunately what usually hangs out is 'the player's pants pockets' - the white flag of surrender".

The psyching effect continues when you make your first bet. Oh, by the way, we don't use real currency to make bets in a casino. Instead, we use casino chips. It's been that way for a long time. Why? Even though it's easier for a dealer to collect losing bets and pay off winning bets with chips rather than currency, casino managers also know that using chips encourages a player to bet more. After all, most players might hesitate putting down a hard earned $25 in bills on the table but these nice looking green casino chips somehow lose their value. They create the illusion that a player isn't really losing anything at all.

To further devaluate the green chips so it doesn't *seem* like you are betting $25, casinos refer to them as "quarter chips" (likewise red $5 are often referred to as "nickels"). Of course, in the mere act of converting cash to chips, Olaf Vancura astutely points out in his book, *Smart Casino Gambling*, "a player psychologically has already been parted with his or her money". He doesn't even get to see where his money went (in the out-of-sight and out-of-mind drop box). The bottom line is that the simple act of converting currency to chips encourages a looser betting style in most players.

What happens when a player gets thirsty while playing? No problem, drinks are on the house! In fact all you can drink is yours for the asking. The fact that it might mar your playing judgment or your ability to act rationally while you are betting your money is *your* problem, not the casinos. It's psychology at its best. After all, have you ever met a player, who's had a few too many, making logical playing and betting decisions? Bottom line is be wary of the "free" drinks. It's just another potential way of casinos psyching players into losing more.

Players get hungry and casinos have a solution for that. It's called the comp. Sure we'll let you eat for free, but only if you keep playing a little while longer. Comps tend to encourage players to play longer and most "free lunches" unfortunately have cost the player dearly. You should by all means get your fair share of comps for your level of betting. Just don't get psyched into betting more or playing longer for the sake of the comp.

You can see the casino's psychological edge in action when you watch what happens to a high roller betting his last chips. A cocktail waitress is usually dispatched to bring him a drink "to make him feel better". His pal, the pit boss, will commiserate with the player telling him he's never seen such bad luck before. "Here", the pit boss says, "go take a break and have dinner and see the show on me. Your luck is bound to change".

After finishing a gourmet meal fit for a king at no cost, our friend enters the show theater (via the "comp line" of course) to a front row seat. Invariably a comedian will make him laugh and he'll soon forget about the thousand dollar bankroll he just blew. After the show, the pit boss arranges a nice room for the evening for his tired and weary friend -on the house, of course. As he dozes off to sleep, he contemplates what a good life this is. And when he awakes, he is refreshed and ready to "beat the tables" because "today will be my lucky day". In less than 24 hours, the casino has psychologically made the player forget his previous day's losses and have what they want - another repeat customer capable of more big losses.

Most players unfortunately go to casinos with an attitude that makes it even easier for casinos to psyche them into losing. Most expect to lose; therefore, it's not too surprising when they achieve their goal. They usually get carried away emotionally, courtesy of the casino environment. Sure they might be conservative back home or at the office, but this is a casino where anything goes. Taking all the free drinks offered by the casinos as a way to getting even for their losses makes sense. And after players lose their bankroll, do they feel sorry for themselves? Hell no! An easier form of denial is to blame their losses on that "rotten luck" or that stupid player or dealer. And to put all the money they lost into perspective, they conclude it was worth it because "they had a good time". They are, in the eyes of the casinos, "happy losers" and they were psyched into accepting their losses in a positive way (by the way, if you think losing money is fun, it ain't nothing compared to the thrill of winning money).

The casino environment also creates "the urge to splurge" in most players. How? Well, if you are treated like royalty, hopefully, you will spend your money like royalty.

You see it all the time. Players like to be called by name by dealers and pit bosses; they enjoy the best food and service; they like being pampered. Couples who hesitate spending a few extra dollars on a dinner or movie back home think nothing of tossing $5 and $10 chips on a gaming table. Making players feel like kings and queens will encourage them to splurge. Not too surprisingly, most do!

The bottom line is that to be a successful casino player, you must not only learn proper playing strategies and sound money management, but you must also learn to control your emotions and prevent the casino's psychological edge to take its toll. The real struggle in most cases is not between you and the casino, but as the high stakes player, author, and publisher, Lyle Stuart, so eloquently put it: "it's between you and yourself".

You will find plenty of temptations to keep you playing and losing in a casino; therefore, you must develop a sense of awareness and self control to overcome the casino's engineered psychological edge. Myron Stabinsky summed it all up when he wrote in his *Zen and The Art of Casino Gambling*: "when we can keep control over our emotions and stay aware of what is happening around us, we can enjoy a safe, highly enjoyable casino experience. However, when we become slaves to negative emotions and allow our egos to cloud our thinking, the luster of excitement quickly turns to something far less pleasant".

So what can you do to avoid being psyched into losing? First of all, when you enter a casino, remember that you are entering a place of business run by very shrewd business people who understand human emotions. Their goal is to separate you from your money as quickly and painlessly as possible and to do so in a way that will make you want to come back and do it again. Go to the casinos with an attitude *that you want to win* rather than the attitude of expecting to lose. Granted, there are no guarantees that you will win, but in an evening of gambling, there is no guarantee that you always have to lose.

Make sure you are mentally alert when you play, go

with a game plan, and set realistic goals. No matter what happens (win or lose), don't let your emotions control you. If you must drink, stick with non alcoholic drinks when you play. Remember casino chips equal your hard earned cash. It's *your* money you are throwing around, not theirs!

Be careful with the easy credit because the casinos would love to extend you some. If you can't handle it, don't use it. Be prepared also for those inevitable losing sessions. Will you call it quits for a day or be like most gamblers and dig in for more cash hoping the tide will turn. Above all, develop the attitude that a small profit at the tables or machines is a lot better than no profit or a loss. After all, you can't be a winner unless you learn to quit a winner.

These attitudes that I'm proposing are not natural and require discipline on your part. Yes, they may take some time until you feel comfortable with them. But if you develop these proper playing attitudes, you will have the mental edge you need to prevent the casino from psyching you into losing.

Attitudes Of Losers	vs	Attitudes of Winners
Expect to lose		Desire to win
Can't wait to gamble		Gambling when alert
Casino time is party time		Have fun, but do the serious playing first
Winning is all luck		Playing skills & mental attitude is important
My luck is bound to change		Learning to set stop losses
I want to win big		Small profits are okay
Take advantage of free drinks		Understand drinking and gambling don't mix
Play for comps		Accept comps for level of play
Feel like a king, spend like a king		It's my hard earned money
So what if I lost, I had fun		Losing isn't fun, winning is

◆ ◆ ◆

Luck vs Skill

When a player wins in a casino, he is most likely to say "I was lucky". Likewise, a losing player chalks up his losses to "bad luck". Although luck is an important factor in determining whether you win or lose at the tables, there is still the element of skill which always overrides the lucky and unlucky cycles that befall a casino player.

As much as most people hate to admit, throughout their lifetime they will have just as many "lucky days" as "unlucky days". Casino players, unfortunately, always remember the unlucky sessions. The times they have a big bet out on the blackjack table, are dealt a 7, 4 and double down only to draw an ace. Unbelievable, but it happens.

There is no question that luck plays an important part in a casino players success. And luck usually runs in cycles. Sometimes you're lucky and you get good cards at the blackjack tables; other times, you get nothing but stiff hands. The casino player must realize that for every unlucky playing session, somewhere, sometime, he will also be blessed with a "lucky" session. So for the moment, it's a fair statement to say that luck will balance out during a casino player's lifetime.

But what about playing and money management skills? Dealers don't possess any of these, only players do. Skill doesn't even out over a lifetime of casino sessions like luck does. Rather, it is something a player always has which overrides the lucky and unlucky sessions.

So how does skill help a player who is having an unlucky, presumably losing session? Skill should enable the player in these circumstances to minimize his losses. And that's important to be a successful casino player because no matter how good a player you are, you will have some losing sessions (remember the lucky-unlucky cycles).

So how does skill help us when we are having a lucky, winning session? By allowing us to maximize our profits. If you are consistently being dealt 11's and 10's in blackjack, you are very lucky. Possessing the skill to know when to double down on these hands will allow you to maximize your profits.

Unfortunately, we can't control when we are going to be lucky or unlucky. This is what makes playing in a casino a gamble. No one can tell before sitting down at a blackjack table or bellying up to a crap table whether or not they will be lucky or unlucky. This is the chance we all take when we gamble in a casino. But we do have control over how skillfully we play. It is this, rather than luck, that separates the losers from the winners.

◆ ◆ ◆

The Ten Commandments of Smart Casino Gambling

Let's be honest. Nobody goes to a casino wanting to lose. Even though it's possible to win, for the majority of players it isn't very probable. The reason is that most players do not really understand the games they play and have never prepared a strategy of where to play, how to play, and most importantly, when to quit.

To help you get started on the road toward being a knowledgeable player, I've prepared the following list of ten commandments for smart casino play. Follow these rules and you'll be improving your chances of winning more and minimize the chances of losing your shirt.

1. Develop a Game Plan

You need to decide which games you are going to play before you head out. Then read up about that game so that you understand the basic rules and know beforehand which are the best bets. Don't depend upon the dealer or fellow player for help. Often their advice is wrong.

2. The Odds Are Against You

The casinos do not depend on the luck of their dealers to stay in business. They have the odds in their favor on virtually every bet. But here is an important point. YOU control the margin of their edge by how well you play. Your goal is to make only bets where the casino's edge is 1.5% or less. The lower the better since this will improve your chances of winning.

3. Don't Drink and Play

There is a reason why alcoholic drinks are free to players. You need to maintain your concentration when you play and alcoholic drinks will dull your thinking. Better to play sober and do your drinking afterwards.

4. Don't Play With Scared Money

You've read this before, but it's worth repeating. Gamble with money you can afford to lose, should the worst happen. Using the rent money to gamble in a casino is one of the biggest mistakes anyone can make. Any gambler who does this needs professional help.

5. Budget Your Money

Always divide your bankroll by the number of playing sessions. If you plan to spend two days gambling, figure on two playing sessions per day. If your total bankroll is $500, then allocate one quarter -or- $125 for each session. Do not, under any circumstances, lose more than your allocated $125 per playing session. This is smart management of your gaming bankroll.

6. Don't Bet More When Losing

When you lose a bet, never increase the size of the next bet to get even. This type of betting can turn into a financial nightmare.

7. Bet More When Winning

Smart players increase their bets gradually when they are winning to take advantage of consecutive wins. This doesn't mean parlaying your winnings. It means adding a portion of your winnings to your next bet and keeping the rest as profits. For example, if you bet $10 and win, set aside $5 as profit and bet $15 on the next hand (or for conservative players, keep $8 and bet $12). This method of betting won't change the casino's edge against you, but will give you the opportunity, if you get lucky, to win a fair amount of money over a short time period.

8. Set A Loss Limit

Always set a limit on the amount you are willing to lose and stick to it! If you can't or won't do this, you will never become a successful casino player.

9. Take The Profits and Run

One of the advantages players have is that we can quit playing anytime we want. When Lady Luck shines on you and you've generated a nice profit, be prepared to quit if the tide turns. Never lose back your hard earned profits. It's your money, not theirs.

10. Set Reasonable Expectations

Sitting down at a blackjack table with a hundred dollar bankroll and expecting to parlay it into a thousand is unrealistic. You will more than likely lose the hundred long before you come close to winning a thousand. Set reasonable win goals. Winning 20 to 50% of your starting bankroll is a good rule of thumb to follow.

Follow these ten commandments and you will be smarter than 99% of the gamblers who play (and constantly lose). I guarantee it!

◆ ◆ ◆

Odds and Probabilities..
What Do They Mean?

The concept of gambling odds and probabilities should be understood by any individual who wants to be a successful casino player.

I don't intend to go into a lengthy mathematical treatise on the subject because I realize most readers find it too difficult and not very entertaining. So, I will try to explain these two terms - odds and probabilities - in a way that's easily understood. Try to follow my explanations and by the time you finish this article, you'll have learned two very important gambling concepts.

I'm sure you've heard the expression "The odds of winning are 6 to 1". What does that mean? Let's focus on the two numbers 6 and 1 in the 6 to 1 term. The 6, which is the first number, is the number of losses which could occur and the second number, the 1, is the number of wins. Thus, if a bet has a 6 to 1 odds, it means that it has 6 chances of losing for every 1 chance of winning.

Let's wander over to the roulette table and calculate the odds of winning a $1 bet on the number 7. First, we must calculate the number of losses or ways to lose on any spin of the roulette wheel. There are 38 numbers on the wheel and you have bet on one of these numbers, the number 7. Therefore, if the roulette ball lands in the number 7 pocket, you win. If it lands in any of the other 37 pockets, you lose. In mathematical terms, the odds of winning are 37 (losses) to 1 (win).

In the above example, you have only one way to win and 37 ways to lose. In a 50/50 game or a game where neither you nor the casino has an edge, the payoff for a winning bet would be 37 to 1. This means for the $1 you bet, you should get back $37 profit. But the casino payoff is 35 to 1, not 37 to 1. In other words, the casinos always pay off winning bets at <u>less</u> than true odds. This is how they stay in business.

Now what about the probability (not odds) of winning a

bet. Take for example the bet on 7 in roulette. Probabilities are expressed as fractions and the numerator of the fraction is the number of wins, the denominator the total number of trials. In the above example, the probability of winning is 1/37.

Probabilities are useful if you want to calculate the chance of a certain event occurring two (or more) times in a row.

For example, what are the chances that number 7 wins two times in a row in roulette? The answer is simply the probability of it occurring once multiplied by the probability of it occurring again. Thus 1/37 x 1/37 = 1/1369. The probability of this occurring is once out of every 1369 trials. So there you have it. Odds is the ratio of losses to wins; probability is the ratio of wins to total trials. When you see a gambling term expressed as "5 to 1", you'll know what it means. You have 5 chances to lose for every 1 chance to win. If instead, someone says the probability of a 7 being tossed on the dice table is 1/6, it means for every six tosses, one should show a 7.

◆ ◆ ◆

Getting Your Fair Share of Comps

A fair amount of questions that I receive from players has to do with comps. For those unfamiliar with the term, a comp is short for complimentary, and it is a way for the casinos to give back something of value for risking your money at the tables (or slots). A comp might be a free meal or discounted or free lodging or even free transportation. In general, the higher your bankroll and betting limits, the higher the value of the comp.

So how do the casinos know how much to give back to the player? And how does a player get a comp? Read on and you will learn the basics of comps.

The casinos use a simple equation to rate a player who plays blackjack, for example. This rating determines how much the casino can expect to win from that player. Based on this calculated expected win, the casinos will usually give back to the player anywhere from 25 to 50% as a comp.

The equation that the casinos use to determine the comp amount is: **Average bet size** times **the number of hands per hour** times **number of hours played** times **casino edge** times **40 percent.**

Suppose you play blackjack with an average bet size of $10. Suppose also that you play blackjack at your favorite casino for 4 hours. On average, you will be dealt 60 hands per hour. Most casinos use 2% as their average edge against the masses of individuals who play blackjack.

If you do the arithmetic, the casinos expect to win $48 from our blackjack player ($10 average bet size times 4 hours times 60 hands per hour times 2 percent casino edge). The casinos are willing to give back 40% of their expected $48 win or $19 in comps.

How does a player get his $19 comp? Simply ask the floor supervisor. In most cases, the player would be given a comp for a meal in a casino restaurant or buffet for a theoretical loss of $19.

Here are some tips for getting the most from the casino's comping policies. You'll get the most returns if you play blackjack skillfully. Why? Because the casinos assume they have a 2% edge against blackjack players. In fact, if you learn the basic playing strategy, the casino's actual edge is only about 0.5%. This means, in our example above, the player's expected loss is a lot less than $48 (actually $12). The smart blackjack player is actually getting $19 worth of comps for an expected loss of only $12. Get the picture?

Comps are not always automatic. The floor supervisors have the freedom to give a comp as they wish (known as the power of the pen). If they are having a bad day, they are usually not liberal giving out comps. As a general rule, women will usually have an easier time getting a comp, especially from a male supervisor.

It's also important to check out the casino's comping policies. Don't expect much in the way of comps from a casino that caters to high rollers vs one that caters to the average or low end player. The easiest way to find this out is to call the casino's marketing department and ask about their comp policies.

One final caution - I've seen too many players betting over their limits just to get a comp. The name of the game is to get your fair share of comps at the level of betting with which you feel comfortable. Do not, I repeat, do not over bet just for the sake of getting a comp! If you want to learn more about comps, I can recommend Max Rubin's book, *Comp City*. Although it contains some controversial advice for getting comps, overall it is the best book on the market explaining what used to be a very secretive part of the casino business.

(Note- See Chapter 4 for a discussion of comps for slot players. Since this article was written, Jean Scott has written an excellent book on comps for low rollers, "The Frugal Gambler.")

◆ ◆ ◆

2

Blackjack

Blackjack Fallacies

A lot of blackjack players have developed certain fallacies about the game. These fallacies seem to perpetuate from one player to another to the point that if a player hears it over and over, it "must be true". Let me try to debunk these fallacies once and for all.

"Blackjack is just a game of luck"

You can say that about any other casino game, but not blackjack. The reason is that once the cards are dealt from the shoe, the odds, or your chances of winning, on subsequently dealt hands is constantly changing. This is not the case with slot machines or roulette or craps. Here the odds are fixed. Past events have no bearing on the future. This is not so with blackjack. You can significantly improve your odds and chances to win by learning the mathematically derived basic playing strategy and better yet, techniques to keep track of the cards as they are played (i.e. card counting).

"You should always insure a good hand"

I had a Las Vegas dealer once tell me this 27 years ago when I first started playing blackjack. Talk about a fallacy that has perpetuated with time. Why do players mistakenly believe in this? Because the casinos give the perception that by making the "insurance" wager, you will be guaranteeing yourself protection against losing a good hand. In actuality, the insurance has nothing to do with your hand. It is simply a side bet you are making with the casino in which you are betting that the dealer's downcard is a ten or picture card (and thus the dealer would have a blackjack hand). Since you have no knowledge whether or not the downcard is a ten value card, it is wise to pass on the insurance bet even with a "good" hand.

"I follow the dealer's playing strategy. After all, he always seems to win."

Players who do this always hit 16 or less and stand on 17 or more, just like the dealer. Seems like the logical thing to do, but there is one catch. In the game of blackjack, the players must act on their hand before the dealer acts on his. And in casinos, if your hand totals greater than 21 (i.e. you bust), you will automatically lose even if the dealer subsequently busts. Therefore following the dealer's rules is a losing strategy.

"A bad player will cause me to lose."

This is probably the most perpetuated fallacy in blackjack. It seems that everyone believes that if a nerdy player hits 16 when the dealer shows a 6 and breaks and then the dealer subsequently makes good, it's the nerd's fault that everyone lost. The plain fact of the matter is that statistically having a player drawing cards when he shouldn't or vice versa will result in no long term change in your expectations. In other words, sometimes a "stupid" play will hurt you and sometimes it will help you. However, if the "stupid" play of a fellow player is really getting to you, then it's time you changed tables.

"The anchor player has the greatest control on whether the dealer will bust."

You will see this fallacy played out every day in casinos. Why? Because the anchor player is the last to act on his hand and all the other players' attention is focused that way. The bottom line is that the anchor player has no more effect on what happens to the dealer hand than any other player on the table. Every play that a player makes will change the order of the cards. It really doesn't matter who draws last or first.

"Pictures follow pictures."

Some players won't hit their stiff hands if they just saw a picture card come out of the shoe. They mistakenly believe that a picture card will always follow another picture card. In fact, once you see a picture card, the probability that the next card will be a picture card is *less*, not more.

"Dealers often cheat at blackjack."

Players who lose usually find excuses for their losses. Why not blame a cheating dealer? The fact of the matter is that dealers in major casinos have no reason to cheat a player. They have too much to lose and very little to gain.

"It's impossible to count cards with 4, 6 or 8 decks of cards."

The reason for this fallacy is that most players believe card counting involves memorizing every card rank as it is dealt from the shoe. This is not true. Card counters assign a number (usually a plus or minus one) to every card and then simply add the plus and minus numbers for every card as it is played. You can count cards just as easily with multiple decks of cards as you can for a single deck.

What are the *facts* of blackjack? For starters, it is far and away your best casino game if you are serious about winning because...

- It is a game of skill, not luck.
- Blackjack players can significantly change the casino's normal edge by how skillfully they play.
- Blackjack players have the potential to turn the tables on the casino and have the edge over them.

Other than high payback video poker machines played perfectly, there is no other casino game that has all of the above characteristics. It stands alone as the casino game that gives players their best shot at winning.

◆ ◆ ◆

Blackjack Advice

I was enjoying myself playing and winning at blackjack when a young lady took a seat next to me. It was obvious after a few hands that she didn't have a clue as to how to play the game so she boldly asked the young dealer for "advice" on how to play her hands. What disturbed me most was that better than half of the advice that he gave her was wrong. Her bankroll rapidly evaporated as she continued to make terrible plays at the advice of the "expert dealer".

I have no grudges to bear against casino dealers. They have a very tough and demanding job. But dealers are trained to deal cards and the vast majority of them have no knowledge of winning blackjack play.

I mentioned the above recent incident because, in fact, I've witnessed an increase in the number of players asking dealers for help in how to play their hands. For some reason, blackjack players believe that if a person deals the game, that person must be an expert on how to play the hands. This, unfortunately, is not true. Most dealers that I've observed know very little about basic strategy and nothing about card counting. Telling players to insure their blackjack hand and never to split a pair of 8's when their upcard is a 10 is simply wrong advice.

The policy in most casinos forbid dealers from advising players whether to hit, stand, double down or pair split. This is for security reasons to prevent any possibility of a dealer and his player friend taking advantage of the casino. However, when novice players openly ask the dealer for advice, they usually respond with a suggested strategy. Often, it's an incorrect strategy.

Dealers aren't the only ones giving misinformation about blackjack playing strategies. I recently picked up a newsletter that was in the racks in one of the Mississippi casinos that offered "helpful hints for table game players from the grand institute of fun and games professor."

On blackjack, the advice was:
1. Split eights unless the dealer shows a ten value card
2. Always split aces
3. Double down on two card combinations of 9, 10, 11
4. Don't take a hit on a possible bust hand (12 or higher) if the dealer's upcard is a 6 or less
5. If you lose more than five times in a row, move to a different table; don't fight the cards.

The first piece of advice is wrong. For every $100 you bet holding a pair of 8's vs a dealer ten upcard, you will on average, gain $5 more by splitting rather than hitting. Standing on a pair of 8's vs a dealer ten value card is an even worse strategy. The bottom line is that a pair of 8's is a bad hand. You should always split 8's against any dealer upcard to get a fair chance at some winning hands. Against a dealer's upcard of 3 and 7, you will usually convert a losing hand into a winning hand by splitting the 8's. In the case of a dealer's upcard of 2, 8, 9, 10 or ace, you will probably lose by splitting, but you lose less over the long run vs standing or hitting.

Always split aces is sound advice. But to double down on two card combinations of 9, 10 and 11 is nonsense unless you specify against which dealer's upcard. The fact of the matter is that you should only double down on two card combinations of 9 if the dealer's upcard is 3, 4, 5 or 6. If the dealer has any other upcard, you should never double down. Likewise, you should double down on two card combinations of 10 only if dealer's upcard is 2 through 9 and double down on 11 only against dealer's upcard of 2 through 10. The above is the mathematically correct doubling strategies for 4, 6 or 8 deck games (with single or double deck games, the doubling strategy is slightly different).

The casino newsletter advises not to take a hit on a possible bust hand (12 or higher) if the dealer's upcard is a 6 or less. The fact of the matter is that the mathematically correct play when you hold a 12 against a dealer's upcard of 2 or 3 is to hit. Although this is a close play, the percentages are still in the favor of hitting 12 on dealer's 2 or 3 and standing on 12 against dealer's 4, 5 or 6.

The point I want to make is that players should not rely on casino generated publications or the advice of dealers to learn blackjack playing strategies. If you have to ask a dealer how to play your hand, then you don't belong on the blackjack table. There are plenty of good books, instructional videos, and even hand-held basic strategy cards that you can take with you on the tables that will give you correct strategies on every hand.

◆ ◆ ◆

You Think You Know How To Play Blackjack?

Okay, so you think you are a hot shot blackjack player? Try this quiz. It will only take a few minutes. Just circle what you believe to be the right answer for each question. You may be surprised at your results.

The game is being dealt with six decks of cards. The rules are: you can double down on any two card combination, doubling is also allowed after you pair split, and the dealer stands on soft 17.

Each question lists the hand dealt to you and the value of the dealer's upcard. You have to decide on the playing strategy. The following abbreviations are used: H is hit, S is stand, D is double, P is split, and Y/N means yes or no. Jot down what you believe to be the correct play and compare with the correct answers that follow.

1. Your hand is Ace, 7. The dealer upcard is a 9.   S H D P
2. Your hand is King, King. The dealer upcard is a 5.   S H D P
3. Your hand is 5, 5. The dealer upcard is a 6.   S H D P
4. Your hand is 10, 2. The dealer upcard is a 2.   S H D P
5. Your hand is 5, 3. The dealer upcard is a 6.   S H D P
6. Your hand is Ace, 3. The dealer upcard is a 3.   S H D P
7. Your hand is 9, 9. The dealer upcard is a 7.   S H D P
8. Your hand is 7, 3. The dealer upcard is a 10.   S H D P
9. Your hand is 10, 6. The dealer upcard is a 7.   S H D P
10. Your hand is ten, ten. The dealer upcard is an   Y N
     Ace and asks you if you want insurance. Do
     you make the insurance bet?

Here are the mathematically correct answers for the above decisions. This is based on simulating the game of blackjack on a computer to determine the best playing decision (which is the one that shows the greatest profit or smallest loss).

1. H	6. H
2. S	7. S
3. D	8. H
4. H	9. H
5. H	10. N

If you got two or more wrong answers, you had better bone up on your blackjack playing strategy before your next casino visit. The following explanation to the above quiz is a good way to start.

1. A soft hand in blackjack is a hand that contains an ace counted as 11. The playing strategies for soft hands are unique. In the case of being dealt an ace, 7 or soft 18, you should double down if the dealer upcard is 3, 4, 5 or 6; you should hit if the dealer upcard is 9, 10 or ace; and stand when the dealer upcard is 2, 7 or 8. Therefore, with the dealer showing a 9, the correct answer is to hit.

2. Whenever you are dealt a pair of picture cards or tens, you have a high potential of winning the hand with your 20. Therefore, never split tens or picture cards; just stand.

3. With a pair of 5's, you can either split them or double down on your total of 10. As a general rule, you should never split 5's. You should double down when the dealer upcard is 2 through 9 and hit if the dealer shows a 10 or ace. With the dealer showing a 6, the correct answer is to double.

4. A 10,2 hand with the dealer showing a 2 is a close call between hitting and standing. The percentages however slightly favor hitting vs standing.

5. In a single deck game, you would double that 5,3 hand against a dealer's 6. But we said this is a six deck game. And in six deck games, you should hit the 5,3 vs doubling.

6. With a soft 14 (ace, 3), you should hit against the dealer's 3. If the dealer instead showed a 5 or 6, then you should double.

7. When you are dealt a pair of nines, you should split when the dealer's upcard is 2 through 9 except against the 7. You have an 18 and against a dealer's 7, you will probably win even if he has a ten downcard. So against the 7, stand vs split.

8. When you are dealt a two card hand that totals ten (such as 7, 3), you should double down when the dealer's upcard is 2 through 9 and hit when the dealer shows a 10 or ace (see question 3 on previous page). The correct answer is to hit your 7, 3 against the 10.

9. A 10, 6 hand is a lousy blackjack hand. Against a dealer's 7 upcard, you will probably lose whether you hit or stand. But over the long haul, the computer results show you will lose less when you hit vs stand. Therefore, the correct play is to hit (and pray!).

10. Making the insurance bet is a bad play unless you are card counting. No matter what you are dealt (yes, even a blackjack hand), you should not make the insurance bet!

If you didn't fare so well on the quiz, I can suggest two choices if you want to continue to play blackjack. Either marry someone who is very wealthy to support your potential losses or take the time and effort to learn the basic playing strategy.

◆ ◆ ◆

The Ten Most Profitable Blackjack Hands

When you play blackjack, you can be dealt many different 2-card hands. For example, you could be dealt an 11 consisting of any one of these 2-card combinations: 2,9; 3,8; 4,7 or 5,6. You could be dealt a hard 17 consisting of either a 10,7 or 9,8. What about being dealt any pair such as 9,9 or a soft hand such as A,6. On the surface, the number of different

2-card combinations seems endless, especially when you consider the card suit and rank of each card.

In actuality, the number of possible 2-card hands can be simplified for two reasons. First, we can eliminate card suits since they have no role in blackjack and secondly, the 10, jack, queen and king can be considered equivalent cards since they all have the value 10. Taking this under consideration, and grouping hands by their different playing strategies, the final number of possible 2-card hands is 33 (note that a pair of 5's is excluded since you should never split 5's).

33 Different 2-Card Player Hands

Hard Hands		Soft Hands	Pairs
5	13	A,2	2,2
6	14	A,3	3,3
7	15	A,4	4,4
8	16	A,5	6,6
9	17	A,6	7,7
10	18	A,7	8,8
11	19	A,8	9,9
12		A,9	10,10
		A,10	A,A

Blackjack theoreticians Braun, Griffin, Revere, Carlson, Chambliss and Rodinski have statistically analyzed and calculated the player's expectation for the 33 hands against every possible dealer upcard. For some of the hands, like 10,10, the player has a positive expectation of winning money against any dealer upcard. With others, like hard 16, the expectation is negative against any dealer upcard. In other hands, like a pair of 9's, the expectation may be positive for some dealer upcards and negative for others.

By ranking the above 33 hands from the largest average positive expectation to the most negative, you arrive at the 10 most profitable blackjack hands.

Ten Most Profitable Blackjack Hands

1. A,10	6. 11
2. A,9	7. A,A
3. 10,10	8. 10
4. A,8	9. 9,9
5. 10,9	10. A,7

The above order of hands will change slightly depending on specific playing rules (whether double after pair splitting is allowed, dealer hits or stands on soft 17, and the number of decks). In any case, it shouldn't come as a surprise that a blackjack hand is the most profitable for players because of the bonus 3 to 2 payout.

If you are wondering why the A,9 is ranked above the 10,10 and the A,8 above the 10,9, it's because the soft hands reduce the dealer's chances of having a blackjack and beating you vs the corresponding hard total.

The calculations that were used to determine the above 10 most profitable blackjack hands assumes that every hand vs all possible dealer upcards is played with the correct basic playing strategy. Misplaying one of these hands could cost you dearly. Therefore, it is important that you learn the correct playing strategy for these hands since they will generate the most profit for you (see table at end of article for the correct basic strategy).

The majority of your total winnings will come from just two hands, A,10 and 10,10, and nearly all the rest of your winnings from these five hands, 11; 10,9; 10; A,9; and A,8. Because a pair of tens is so profitable, it should never be split - a mistake often made by novice players (note: card counters sometimes split 10's, but only when the remaining cards are rich in tens and aces). Standing on a soft total of 20 is also a sure winner. If you remember anything from this article, remember this: STAND WHEN YOU ARE DEALT ANY 20!

If you are not dealt your fair share of these 10 most profitable hands the next time you play blackjack, then don't be too surprised if you find yourself losing. On the other hand, you stand a good chance of walking away from the tables a winner if the reverse occurs and you play these hands correctly. This is why it is so important to learn the correct basic playing strategy for them.

Early in my blackjack career, a professional player posed this question to me. Suppose the casino lets you have an automatic 18 on every hand dealt to you; would you sit down and play? My response at that time was "yes" since I thought I couldn't lose with an 18 on every hand. Well, guess what? For every 100,000 hands of 18 dealt to you, overall you will lose 28 more hands than you will win. In other words, 18 is an overall losing hand in blackjack. This is why 18 doesn't appear as one of the 10 most profitable blackjack hands.

The above only holds for hard 18. If you are dealt a soft 18 hand (Ace,7), you have the possibility of taking another card to try to improve the hand without busting. You'll lose less over the long run when you hit soft 18 against a dealer upcard of 9, 10 or Ace rather than stand. When the dealer shows a weak 3, 4, 5 or 6, you will make more money by doubling down vs hitting or standing. Against a dealer's 2, 7 and 8, the better play is to stand with the 18.

Likewise, most players are happy to stand on a 17. Unfortunately, a 17 is also an overall losing hand. The alternative strategy of hitting hard 17 would only increase your losses. With soft 17, on the other hand, you should hit (and sometimes double down) to try to improve your total since you can not bust by drawing one card. A simple rule to remember is NEVER STAND ON SOFT 17.

On average, you will win about 43% of all blackjack hands dealt to you, lose about 47% of the hands and tie 9%. If we discount the ties, you can expect to win 47% of the hands and lose 53%. How is it possible to end up a winner when you lose more hands than you win? This is because for most of your winning (i.e. profitable) hands, you will be getting paid either 1½ times your initial bet (for blackjack hands) or double your initial bet (when doubling down or pair splitting on hands such as 11; A,A; 10; 9,9; and A,7). With losing hands you will most likely be betting and losing only your initial wager. In other words, you win more money from the 47% of the hands you win than the amount you lose from the 53% losing hands.

Basic Playing Strategy For The
10 Most Profitable Blackjack Hands
(multiple deck, double after pair splitting allowed, dealer stands on soft 17)

A,10; A,9; 10,10; A,8; 10,9   **ALWAYS STAND**

11   **Double down** on dealer's 2 through 10 and **hit** if dealer shows Ace.

A,A   **ALWAYS SPLIT** (some casinos also allow resplit of aces)

10 (including 5,5)   **Double down** on dealer's 2 through 9 and **hit** if dealer shows 10 or Ace

9,9   **Split** if dealer shows 2 through 6 plus 8 and 9. **Stand** if dealer shows 7, 10 or Ace

A,7   **Double down** on dealer's 3 through 6, hit on dealer's 9, 10, Ace and **stand** on dealer's 2, 7 and 8

(Note: For single deck games where doubling after pair splitting is not allowed, you should double down on 11 vs Ace, Ace,8 vs 6 and 9 vs 2.)

The Ten Least Profitable Blackjack Hands

Ever wonder what are the 10 least profitable blackjack hands even when they are played with the correct basic strategy? Here they are with a hand of 16 being the worst.

1.	hard 16	6.	hard 17
2.	hard 15	7.	6
3.	hard 14	8.	5
4.	hard 13	9.	7
5.	hard 12	10.	6,6

You will lose on average about 16 to 42 cents per $100 bet on these hands. In fact, just 6 of those hands - hard 12 through 17 - will account for about 80% of your financial losses. So why would you follow the basic strategy for these hands when financially you stand to lose money? Because if you play by any other strategy, you will most likely lose much more over the long run. The basic playing strategy allows you to minimize your losses with these poor player hands. "Losing less" is an important concept in blackjack and Julian Braun, world renown blackjack authority, put it best when he stated:

"You will have your share of stiffs. If you find a way to lose less of those than otherwise, the "less" becomes a gain. Contrarily, you will have your share of winning hands. If you can find a way of "winning more" when you do have such winning hands, that too is a gain. It is the ability to play for these extra gains that makes a tough successful player."

◆ ◆ ◆

Stand or Hit... Your Decision

Of all the playing decisions you must make at the blackjack table, the decision to stand or take a hit will occur most frequently. Understanding when to hit those 12 to 16 hands and when not to will often be the difference in leaving the tables a winner or loser.

First, let's take a look at the dealer's situation. We know by the rules of the game, dealers must always hit when the total of their hand is 16 or less and they must stand if their hand totals 17 through 21. This is an automatic play on their part regardless of the total of the players' hands. For example, if a player stands on a hand that totals 15 and the dealer has a higher hand of 16, the dealer must still draw a card or hit.

Notice in the above example, the player stood on a 15. That's one of the advantages players have in blackjack. We don't have to hit 15's or for that matter any hand. Therefore, to aid us in the decision of whether to stand or hit, it would be nice if we know how many times the dealer will break or exceed 21 for every upcard he could be dealt. After all, if we know the dealer had a high probability of busting, we would be foolish to hit our 12 through 16 hands and risk busting. Especially since we must play out our hands before the dealer and if we bust, we automatically lose our bet even if the dealer subsequently busts.

Fortunately for blackjack players, the probability of the dealer busting for each upcard can be computed using high speed computers that simulate the game. The results are:

Dealer's upcard	2	3	4	5	6	7	8	9	10	Ace
Percent Bust	35	37	40	42	42	26	24	23	23	17

The above gives us a clear indication of the probability of the dealer busting. When the dealer's upcard is 5 or 6, for example, he has a 42% chance of busting or about 4 out of 10 times. These are his worst upcards. Likewise, the dealer's probability of busting is relatively high with a 2, 3 or 4 upcard and relatively low with 7, 8, 9, 10 or Ace. The dealer is less likely to bust with an Ace upcard.

With the above information, we should logically be able to figure out whether we should hit or stand. Let's take two cases: the times we are dealt the poor totals of 12 through 16 and the times we are dealt the rather good hands of 17 through 21. To make this less complicated, let's assume for the moment that we are only discussing hands that either don't contain an ace or, if the ace is present, it has the value of one (these are known as hard hands).

If you are dealt a 12 through 16 and the dealer has a low value upcard (2 through 6), we know the dealer has a high probability of busting. In this situation, we would be foolish to take a hit because if we bust we automatically lose. The best strategy in this situation is to stand and not draw cards; instead, letting the dealer hit in a situation where his probability of busting is high.

On the other hand, if we are dealt a 12 through 16 and the dealer has a relatively low probability of busting (upcard of 7 through ace), then our strategy needs to be more aggressive and we should hit our hand, hoping to improve our total to at least 17.

The above rules can be summarized as follows. If the dealer has a low value upcard (2 through 6), then you should stand on low totals (12 through 16). If the dealer has a high value upcard (7 through ace), then you should hit your low totals (12 through 16). And finally, if you are dealt a 17 through 21, then regardless of the dealer's upcard, you should always stand because your probability of busting is much too high if you were to hit.

The one exception to the above rules which you need to learn is the situation in which you are dealt a 12 and the dealer's upcard is a 2 or 3. Mathematically, it's a very close call whether to stand or hit, but the very slight edge goes to hitting.

Now what about standing or hitting hands that contain an ace counted as 11. These are known as soft hands. For example, Ace, 3 is a soft 14; Ace, 6 is a soft 17. These hands must be considered differently because of the dual role of the ace (it can either count as 11 or 1). Likewise, a player can never draw a card to a soft hand and bust. For example, if the player had a soft 15 (A,4) and drew an 8, the ace can be counted as 1 and the player has a total of 13.

As a general rule, you should always stand on soft 19, 20 and of course, 21 (the latter is a blackjack). You should never stand on soft 17 or less hands. In fact, the better play to make with soft hands is to double down in certain situations. The optimum playing strategy for soft hands is as follows.

soft 19, 20	stand
soft 18	double on 3,4,5,6;
	hit on 9,10, ace
	stand on 2,7 and 8
soft 17	double on 3,4,5,6;
	hit on 2,7,8,9,10, ace
soft 16 and 15	double on 4,5,6;
	hit on 2,3,7,8,9,10, ace
soft 14 and 13	double on 5,6;
	hit 2,3,4,7,8,9,10, ace

Notice that most of the double down situations occur when the dealer has a high probability of busting (low value upcards). One simple rule to remember is when the dealer's upcard is 5 or 6, always double down on soft 13 through 18.

When you hit a soft hand, it sometimes converts to a hard hand, which means you have to switch from soft hand to hard hand playing strategy. For example, suppose you are dealt an ace, 4 vs a dealer's 7 upcard. You should hit the soft 15 hand. Assume you drew a 9. Your three card hand is now a hard 14 (ace, 4, 9). You should now use the hard hand playing strategy which in this case dictates hitting the 14 vs the 7 upcard.

If you follow the above rules for standing, hitting (and doubling on soft hands), you won't win every hand, but you'll always be making the mathematically correct play that will maximize your long term profits and minimize your losses. That's the smart way to play blackjack!

◆ ◆ ◆

Doubling Down
A Smart Blackjack Play

Blackjack players have certain playing options available to them. One of the most important is knowing when to double down.

When playing blackjack, you have the option of doubling down after you receive your initial two cards. This option allows you to double your bet in favorable situations in return for receiving one and only one draw card. Doubling down, for example, on a two card total of 11 is a smart strategy since your chances of drawing a ten for a 21 are good (there are 16 ten value cards per deck). Doubling down allows you to double your bet when your chances of beating the dealer are good.

There are some basic rules associated with doubling down. First you can only double down after you receive your initial two cards. In other words, if you decide to take a hit and draw a third card, you can no longer double down. This is a rule in effect in virtually every casino (however, recently some casinos are allowing players the option to double down on 2, 3 and 4 cards). Also, most casinos allow a player to double down on any two initial cards. Some, notably casinos in northern Nevada and in the Caribbean, restrict doubling to two card hands that total 9, 10 and 11. You are much better off when a casino does not restrict the hands that you can double down.

A most favorable option is to be allowed to double down after you pair split. For example, if you split a pair of sixes and draw a 4 to the first six, you would be permitted to double down (after you split). Likewise if you drew a 5 to the other six, you would have the option to double down again.

To exercise the double down option, you simply place an equivalent amount of chips next to your original bet on the layout. Do not place your chips on top of the original bet. When you position your chips next to your original bet, the dealer understands you want to double down and will give you one and only one draw card. No matter what the value of the draw card, you are not permitted to ask for additional draw cards after exercising the double down option.

Some casinos allow players to double down for less than their original bet as long as the player meets the minimum bet requirement posted on the table. For example, if you bet $10 at a $5 minimum game, you could double for $5. As a general rule, if you learned the correct playing strategy for doubling down, you should always do so for the maximum amount rather than for less.

The determination of the correct double down playing strategy is done by computer simulating a particular hand vs a specific dealer upcard then comparing the results of doubling vs an alternate strategy (e.g. hitting) for millions of hands. The results of this analysis yield the mathematically correct strategy for doubling down.

For casinos that use multiple decks and allow doubling down after pair splitting, you should double down as follows:

Double hard 11 (e.g. 8, 3) when dealer's upcard is 2 through 10.
Double hard 10 (e.g. 6, 4) when dealer's upcard is 2 through 9.
Double hard 9 (e.g. 6, 3) when dealer's upcard is 3 through 6.

For soft hands, mainly those two card hands that contain the ace, you should double as follows:

Double down on A,6 and A,7 when dealer's upcard is 3 through 6.
Double down on A,4 and A,5 when dealer's upcard is 4 through 6.
Double down on A,2 and A,3 when dealer's upcard is 5 or 6.

The above double down strategy is slightly modified for casinos that do not allow doubling after pair splitting and also for casinos that deal single and double deck games. However, the above strategy is a close approximation to get you started at cutting the odds in blackjack.

For most of the hands that you will be dealt in blackjack, you will be in a losing posture because the dealer will have the better chance of winning. In these instances we play defensively trying to minimize our loss in a losing situation. With doubling down, we take the offensive. The only time you should double is when your chances of winning the hand are better than the dealer's or you stand to earn more profit by doubling vs hitting the hand. Doubling down is one of our offensive strategies that allows us to put more money on the table when our chances of winning are good. To pass up the opportunity to do so is like handing over your money to the casino.

◆ ◆ ◆

Should I Split The Pair or Not?

An important player option in blackjack is to split pairs. This is especially so in casinos that allow the favorable rule of doubling down after pair splitting. The point of this article is to go over the basics of pair splitting so you will understand what it is and how and when to do it.

If the initial two cards dealt to you have the same value, such as a pair of 8's, you may split the hand into two hands. Statistically you can expect to receive a pair about 14% of the hands dealt to you, which is on the average, 14 hands out of every 100. However, only 2 of the 14 pair of hands should be split.

In games in which players are *not* permitted to touch the cards, which is the norm for multiple deck games dealt from a playing shoe, the proper way to split is to simply place the same value chip(s) next to (not on top!) the original wager in the betting circle. Do not separate or touch the cards; the dealer will do this.

In hand-held games (normally games dealt with a single or double deck of cards), you pair split by placing your cards face up on the table above your wager and then make the secondary wager next to your initial wager.

When you pair split, you have converted the initial hand into two independent hands and also doubled your bet. Each of the two split hands must be played separately. Should you receive a card of like value to the initial two split cards, most casinos will allow you to resplit a third and if it happens again, a fourth time. For example, if you split a pair of 6's and draw another 6 to the first hand, you may make another wager and split the 6's again. In this case, the player would have three hands with three wagers, each hand starting with a 6 upcard.

You may request as many draw cards as you wish to each split hand until you are satisfied with the total for the hand. The exception is splitting aces. Most casinos will only permit one draw card to each split ace. However, recently more and more casinos are giving players a break and allowing them to resplit aces.

Mechanically, the first decision you should make as a player is to decide whether or not to split. This takes precedence over standing, hitting or doubling. You look at your initial two cards and you either have two like cards (a pair) or not. If you do not have a pair, case is closed and you don't worry about whether or not to split. If instead you have a pair, you now focus on the value of the dealer's upcard. It's these two variables - the value of your pair and the value of the dealer's upcard that determines whether you split or not.

During my 27 years of playing blackjack, I have observed players split every conceivable pair regardless of what the dealer's upcard is. The absolute worst play is to split 10's or picture cards (unless you are card counting). If you are dealt a pair of 10's, you have 20, which more than likely is a winning hand. Do not, I repeat, do not split those 10's! Also, remember to never split a pair of 5's. You are much better off playing the pair of 5's as a single hand with a total of 10, than to split the 5's.

On the other hand, you should always split aces and 8's. Even if the dealer shows an ace or 10 upcard, you are still better off in the long run to split the 8's and aces. You won't win every split hand, but in the long run, you will win more money by <u>always</u> splitting aces and 8's.

As a general rule, you should split pairs when the dealer has a low value upcard (7 or less). Grouping the pairs will make it easier to learn the rules for when to split. For example, in multiple deck games in which the casinos allow doubling down after pair splitting, you should split 2's, 3's and 7's when the dealer's upcard is 2 through 7. Just remember the 2 to 7 spread on pairs of 2's, 3's and 7's.

Learning the rule for splitting 6's is also easy. It's not on dealer's 2 through 7, but dealer's 2 through 6. Remember the rule: You split 6's on 2 through 6.

You should only split 4's when the dealer's upcard is 5 or 6. Remember the sequence 4, 5 and 6. Splitting 9's is probably the hardest rule to remember. You should split 9's when the dealer's upcard is 2 through 9 with one exception - when the dealer shows a 7. Why not split in this situation? You are holding a hand that totals 18 and if you assume the dealer has a ten hole card, he has 17. Your 18 will beat his 17, therefore, you should not split.

It's important to remember that pair splitting is in most cases a defensive strategy in which you are trying to cut your losses rather than to win more money. I realize it is a hard concept for most players to understand, namely doubling your bet in order to lose less on two hands than you would have lost on the one hand. But if you do the mathematics, this is indeed the case on most pair splits. There are exceptions. For example, splitting aces (except against a dealer's ace) and 9's (vs dealer's 2 through 6 and 8) are two categories of pair splitting decisions in which a player will turn an overall losing situation into a winning one.

Basic strategy players are not the only kind of players that benefit from the pair splitting rules. Card counters are also more likely to pair split in a high count situation in which they have wagered a big bet (because they have the edge on the next deal). By pair splitting, the counter will either turn a losing situation into a winning one or cut his losses. Also, counters will sometimes split hands in high counts that you would not ordinarily do. For example, if the count gets high enough indicating there are a lot of 10's and aces still left in the undealt cards, a counter sometimes may split 10 value cards in the hopes of drawing a 10 or ace.

The table below summarizes the correct pair splitting rules for single, double and multiple deck games with doubling after pair splitting. For other rule variations that may require modifying the pair splitting rules, please consult the strategy tables in my book, *Blackjack: Take The Money and Run.*

Pair splitting is a favorable player option in blackjack, but only when you learn how to properly use it. Be a smart player and learn the correct pair splitting strategies and you will be improving your chances of winning.

PAIR SPLITTING STRATEGIES

The correct strategies for pair splitting in single deck games with doubling after pair splitting allowed are:

> always split aces and 8's
> split 2, 3, 6's vs dealer's upcard of 2 through 7
> split 4's vs dealer's upcard of 4, 5 and 6
> split 7's vs dealer's upcard of 2 through 8
> split 9's vs dealer's upcard 2 through 6, 8 and 9
> never split a pair of 5's or 10's

For 2, 4, 6 and 8 deck games in which the casino allows doubling after pair splitting, modify the above as follows:

split 4's vs dealer's upcard of 5 and 6
split 6's vs dealer's upcard of 2 through 6
split 7's vs dealer's upcard of 2 through 7

◆ ◆ ◆

Surrender or Die!

More casinos in Vegas and elsewhere are offering the surrender rule at blackjack. Like most player options in blackjack, if you know when to use it correctly, it can be to your advantage. On the other hand, if you misuse the option, it's like throwing money down the drain.

First, an explanation of what surrender is all about since it is not a very popular option in blackjack. After a player receives his initial two cards, he may at his discretion surrender the hand. When a player tells the dealer he wants to "surrender", the dealer will remove the player's cards from the table and 50% of his bet. In essence, the player has forfeited his chance to play out the hand and the casino keeps one-half of the bet.

"Wait a minute! Who in his right mind would "give up" half of his bet without playing out his hand? Seems like a cowardly thing to do at the blackjack tables. How are you supposed to win when you give the casino half of your bet? Seems like a crazy playing option you would only see the uninformed tourist doing". If thoughts like this raced through your mind, read on and you will be surprised to learn that both the casino and player profit from this new option.

From the player's perspective, when is it the best time to surrender? It seems logical that you should only surrender a hand when your chances of winning that hand are not very good. After all, it's better to *save* half of your bet than to lose it all.

Let's take a look at what the odds are of winning one of the worst player hands in blackjack - a 16 - when the dealer's upcard is a 10. If you analyze this hand over and over using a blackjack computer software program, you'll find that you will lose over the long run about 77% of the hands when you hit. That means you will win about 23% of the hands. If you wager a buck a hand and lose 77 hands and win 23 hands, you would be down $54. But what about standing on that 16 rather than hitting? You'll actually do a tad bit worse, but if you round the numbers, you end up still losing about the same - $54.

Now, let's look at what happens if you surrender the hand. If you bet a buck a hand and surrender, you get back 50 cents. If you do it over 100 hands, you'll end up losing $50. Compare this with the $54 you can expect to lose by either hitting or standing on that 16. Get the point? By surrendering, you can cut your loss by $4 in a losing situation.

The bottom line is that you should only surrender blackjack hands when your chances of winning are less than 25% (this means the casino has a greater than 50% chance of beating you). If the casino's edge is greater than 50%, then you are better off to surrender half (or 50%) of your bet.

When you are playing in multiple deck blackjack games, you should only surrender these hands: 16 when the dealer shows a 9, 10 or ace; a 15 when the dealer shows a 10. Do not surrender a pair of 8's and never surrender a soft 15 or 16 (that's a hand which contains an ace counted as 11-like ace, 5). In two deck games, you should only surrender a 15, 16 and pair of 7's against a dealer's 10.

The casinos make a lot of money with the surrender rule from players who surrender hands when they shouldn't. I observed a player making a $25 bet and surrendering a 12 against a dealer's 10. This was literally throwing money at the casinos by surrendering that hand (the proper strategy was to hit).

Surrender is a unique blackjack option. It's the only option that you must verbally communicate to the dealer (certainly not the case with hitting or standing). Also remember that if you were to ask for a third card draw, the surrender option is no longer available. And finally if the dealer has a blackjack, you can not surrender (if the dealer turns over a blackjack, all player hands lose).

Mathematically, surrender will cut the casino's edge by about 0.05%. It doesn't seem like much, but your objective should be to play as smart as possible to cut the casino's edge to as low as possible. Taking advantage of the surrender rule will help you achieve this objective.

The surrender rule on the previous page is known as late surrender since you can't surrender your hand if the dealer turns over a blackjack hand. Another type of surrender exists which allows a player the option to surrender even if the dealer turns over a blackjack hand. This option is known as early surrender and it was popular during the beginning of legalized casino gambling in Atlantic City (the rule was subsequently revoked).

Early surrender is a very favorable player option that can add 0.6% in the player's favor. Unfortunately, nowadays, not so many casinos allow it. But from time-to-time, a few casinos will offer it as a special promotion to attract new business. The correct early surrender playing strategy for multiple deck games is to surrender these initial 2 card hands.

Player Hand	Dealer Upcard
17	ace
16	10, ace
15	10, ace
14	10, ace
13	ace
12	ace
7	ace
6	ace
5	ace

Do not surrender soft hands

Don't think of surrender as "giving away half of your bet". When you use it correctly, you will instead be *saving* half of your bet.

(Note: Since this article was written, Arnold Snyder, in his book, "Blackjack Wisdom"; came up with a marvelously simple rule on when to surrender a hand. Surrendering half your bet is the optimal strategy decision only if you will lose more than three times as many hands as you will win. If you stand to win 23% of the hands and lose 77%, you should surrender since 77% is more than three times 23%.)

◆ ◆ ◆

Insurance Anyone?

A popular blackjack playing option is to buy insurance. We are not talking about car or home insurance, but rather a side bet that players can make whenever the dealer's upcard is an ace. Is it a smart bet? Who has the odds? What about insuring a player's blackjack? Read on.

First, let's explain the rules and mechanics of the insurance bet. Whenever the dealer's upcard is an ace, the dealer will interrupt the game and ask all players if they want to take (or buy) insurance. Basically, the dealer is asking if you want to bet that his downcard is a ten value card. If it is, the dealer would have a blackjack hand and you would lose your bet for the hand (unless you had a blackjack), but you would win your insurance bet at a 2 to 1 payoff.

The amount you can wager on the insurance bet is equal to one half of the amount of your initial wager on the hand. Thus, if you had a ten dollar initial wager, you could make a five dollar insurance wager.

There is a place on the blackjack layout known as the insurance line (right above where you make your initial bet). Here is where you place your chip(s) for the insurance bet.

Once all players are given the opportunity to make the insurance bet, the dealer will announce that insurance is closed and then check his downcard to determine if it is a ten value card.

In some casinos, the dealer will carefully peek at the downcard by physically bending the corner of the card and peeking at it in a manner that will not reveal the value of the card to any player. You can imagine what kind of an edge a player would have if he had knowledge of the downcard (assuming it wasn't a ten value card). Many casinos have adopted a special viewer on the table that allows the dealer to slip the downcard face down into the viewer and determine, without bending the edge of the card and peeking, whether the downcard is a ten value card. This device eliminates any possibility of cheating by either the player or dealer.

When the dealer's downcard is a ten value card and he has blackjack, the dealer will immediately turn over the downcard and then pay all the player's insurance bets at 2 to 1 payoff (thus a five dollar insurance wager will win ten dollars). Since the dealer has a blackjack hand, all of the initial player bets on the hand are lost (except player blackjacks).

If instead, the dealer asks for insurance and doesn't have a ten value downcard, the dealer will immediately collect all player's insurance wagers (since the dealer did not have the blackjack, all insurance bets lose). After the dealer collects the losing insurance bets, he will continue with the round.

As a general rule, insurance is a bad bet. You will lose more money making the insurance bet than you will win. In fact, in a single deck game, for example, you will lose an average of 5.8% of all the money you bet on insurance. The odds are against you, therefore, you should pass up the insurance bet when it is offered.

Now what about the special case when you are dealt a blackjack, the dealer has an ace upcard and asks insurance? Most players will gladly take the insurance because whether the dealer does or does not have a blackjack, the player is guaranteed a 1 to 1 overall payoff. In fact, most casinos will allow a player to "take even money" in this situation. What this means is that the dealer will automatically pay you 1 to 1 for your blackjack. Taking even money is the same as going through the motions of making an insurance bet when you have a blackjack, only it eliminates a lot of time and work on the part of the dealer (just say "yes" to even money and you are paid on the spot).

Unfortunately, most blackjack players mistakenly believe taking even money is a smart play because you automatically win even money regardless of whether or not the dealer's downcard is a ten value card. The bottom line, however, is that mathematically you will be giving away, on average, about 4% of your profits to the casino each time you take even money (or make the insurance bet) when you have blackjack.

Trust me, this game is tough enough to beat without looking for ways to shortchange yourself on blackjack hands. Do not make the insurance bet or take even money when you are dealt a blackjack hand. Unless you have been tracking the cards that have been played (i.e. card counting), you have no knowledge of the probability that the dealer's downcard is a ten value card. Card counters, on the other hand, have this knowledge and therefore the insurance bet is a potential money maker for them. So, unless you are counting, do not - I repeat - do not make the insurance bet or take even money unless you like giving your money away to casinos!

◆ ◆ ◆

How To Remember The Basic Playing Strategy

Has this ever happened to you? You make a $5 bet and are dealt an ace and a 6. The dealer shows a 7 upcard. Before you know it, the dealer is pointing in your direction waiting for a signal from you on whether or not you want another card or want to stand. You've reviewed the basic playing strategy over and over, but now in the "heat of the battle", your mind goes blank and you can't remember the right strategy. You guess and stand on the 17 (which turns out to be the wrong play - you should have hit the hand).

It's one thing to learn the basic strategy and quite another to remember it during the excitement of playing blackjack. But perhaps the technique of using a flow chart will help.

The flow chart will force you into an organized, logical thinking process to arrive at the correct basic strategy play for any given hand and dealer upcard. I assume you have some knowledge of the basic strategy. What I will show you is the logical thinking process you can use to help yourself arrive at the correct play.

The thinking process you should follow starts with whether or not you should surrender, then whether or not to pair split, then whether or not to double down, and finally whether or not to stand or hit. Remember SURRENDER, PAIR SPLIT, DOUBLE DOWN, STAND/HIT, in that sequence. In practice, your thinking process should work like this.

After you receive your 2 cards, decide whether or not to surrender your hand (note: some casinos do not offer surrender). The key card for this decision is the dealer's upcard. If the dealer has a 9, 10 or ace upcard, then you need to determine whether or not to surrender in accordance with the basic strategy rules for surrendering. If the dealer does not have a 9, 10 or ace upcard, then your decision on whether or not to surrender is NO.

If you don't have the correct hand to surrender (in multiple deck games, only hard 15 and 16 hands should be surrendered, but not 8, 8) or the dealer doesn't show a 9, 10 or ace upcard, then proceed to the next decision - whether or not to pair split.

Obviously, if you do not have a pair, your decision is NO to pair splitting. If you have a pair, then you would split in accordance with the basic strategy rules for pair splitting. If you end up not pair splitting because you either don't have a pair or the basic strategy tells you not to split a pair vs a specific dealer upcard, then proceed to the next decision - whether or not to double down.

The key for doubling is the player hands of hard 9, 10 and 11 and the soft hands 13 through 18 (that's hands that contain an ace counted as 11; like ace, 6 or soft 17 hand). These are the only hands that a player should ever double down in a multiple deck game. If you have one of these hands, then you should double down according to the basic strategy rules for doubling. If you don't have one of these hands, then your decision is NO to doubling.

After you've logically decided on whether to surrender, pair split and double down, your last decision is whether or not to stand or hit in accordance with the basic strategy rules. Let's try a few examples so you get the hang of how easy this technique is.

Suppose you are dealt a 10, 6 and the dealer's upcard is a 6. First decision is surrender? Answer - NO (because you would never surrender hard 16 against a dealer 6). Next decision is pair split? Answer is NO (because you don't have a pair). Double down? Answer - NO (because you don't have one of the listed player hands for doubling). Your final decision is whether or not to stand or hit (in accordance with basic strategy, you should stand on this hand).

How about if you are dealt a 9, 9 and dealer shows an 8. Go through the logical decision making process. Surrender? NO, because dealer doesn't show a 9, 10 or ace. Pair split? Possibly because you have a pair (of 9's). By the basic strategy rules for pair splitting, you should split the 9's against the dealer's 8 upcard.

What if you were dealt an ace, 2 and the dealer showed a 2 upcard? Surrender? NO, because the dealer doesn't show a 9, 10 or ace. Pair split? NO, because you don't have a pair. Double down? Possibly because you have a soft 13; one of the hands you could double down. But according to the basic strategy, you double down on soft 13 only when the dealer shows a 5 or 6 upcard. Since the dealer shows a 2 upcard, in accordance with basic strategy, you should hit.

Practice following this decision making, logical flow to determine how to play your hand. Just remember the sequence: SURRENDER, PAIR SPLIT, DOUBLE DOWN, STAND/HIT. Always start by first determining whether or not to surrender and if the decision is NO, go to the next decision of pair splitting and so forth. If you get in the habit of following this flow, you will be surprised at how easy it is to determine how to play your hand the next time you play blackjack.

◆ ◆ ◆

Blackjack Side Bets ... A Good Deal or Not?

Most casinos offer several different types of bonuses and options at their blackjack table. This is done to stimulate more interest in the game. Some of these bets have a relatively high casino edge while others can actually make money for a skillful player. Let's sort out these side bets and determine the good from the not-so-good. The mathematical analysis of most of these side bets and bonuses was done by Donald Schlesinger and appears in detail in his outstanding book, *Blackjack Attack*.

Winning Suited 6, 7, 8

Whenever a player is dealt a 6, 7 and 8 of the same suit and it's a winning hand, a player receives a bonus payoff of 2 times the original bet. The best playing strategy is to actually follow the basic strategy, except in one instance. You should only deviate from basic strategy if you are dealt a 6,7 of the same suit and the dealer's upcard is a 2. Even with this one deviation, this rule is not worth much to a player (about an extra penny per $100 wagered) because the probability of getting a 6, 7, 8 suited is very low.

Winning 7, 7, 7

If you are dealt three consecutive 7's, the bonus payoff in some casinos is 3 to 2. Unfortunately, the frequency of being dealt three 7's is very small. Your gain is about the same as for 6, 7, 8 suited, about a penny per $100 wagered. Do not deviate from basic strategy. Even if you are dealt two 7's and the dealer shows a low value upcard, you should split the 7's per the basic strategy rules rather than go for broke and hit in an attempt to draw the third 7.

5-Card 21

Also known as the 5-card Charlie rule, some casinos will pay a player a 2 to 1 bonus if they have a winning hand that totals 21 in 5 cards. This bonus gives the player an extra 0.2% edge. However, there are some 24 changes to the basic strategy rules which should be implemented in an attempt to obtain the 5-card Charlie. Some of these strategy deviations include hitting a 4 card 14 vs dealer's 2, and 4 card 13 vs 2, 3, 4 and 6. Also, you should hit soft 18 vs 2 through 8.

Over/Under Proposition

This side bet is clearly labeled on the layout. A player who bets the over is betting that his two cards will total over 13. If it does, the player wins the side bet. If it totals less than 13, the bet is lost. Likewise, betting on the under wins if a player's first two cards total 12 or less. If a player receives a two card hand that totals exactly 13, both the over and under bets are lost.

This side bet is not a good bet for the basic strategy player. The casino's edge is close to 6.6% on the over and a whopping 10% on the under. However, for players who keep track of cards as they are played (i.e. card counters), the over/under bet can be a very favorable bet giving the skillful counter about a 1.5 to 2.0% edge. But you must learn specific card counting strategies for this side bet to obtain this potential edge.

Super 7's

This side bet wins if a player gets any one of a number of 7's. A typical payoff for a dollar bet is: three 7's on the first 3 cards pays $5,000, two suited 7's on first 2 cards pays $100; two 7's of any suit pays $50 and a 7 on the first card pays $1. The enticement of this side bet is the rather high potential payoff for a dollar bet. However, when you do the math, the bottom line is that the casinos have a rather large edge over players (about 11%).

Resplitting Aces

In the old days, if you split aces, the casino would only allow one draw card per ace. If you drew another ace, you would be stuck with a two card 12. Nowadays, many casinos allow you to resplit aces. If you split aces and draw another ace, you can resplit again. This is a favorable player rule adding about 0.05% edge to the player.

Dealer Hits Soft 17

In some casinos, a dealer must hit his soft 17 hand, rather than stand. This is not a player favorable rule. It costs a player about 0.2%. You are better off playing where the casino rule mandates the dealer to stand on all soft 17's.

The world of blackjack is ever changing with new options, bonuses and rules appearing. Before you make any side bet on a blackjack table or change your playing strategy because of a new playing option or bonus payoff, make sure you know beforehand whether it's worth your while.

Basics of Blackjack Card Counting

Blackjack card counting is a playing strategy that can

give a player a slight mathematical advantage over the casino. In other words, a player who accurately card counts stands to win, rather than lose, more money playing blackjack over an extended period of time. However, this does not mean blackjack card counters win every time they play. In fact, it's quite the contrary. Because of the variability in the game, blackjack card counters experience normal fluctuations in their bankroll. What this means is that sometimes their bankroll increases as they experience winning sessions; other times, their bankroll decreases when no matter how well they play, they lose. Think of it as a roller coaster ride. I have personally lost ten consecutive times, yet I've won more money than I've lost over 27 years of playing blackjack. These positive and negative bankroll fluctuations are inherent in the game of blackjack and in a future article, I will explain why this is so. For now, I just wanted you to be aware of this fact before I explain what card counting is all about.

A player who card counts is watching all the cards as they are dealt on the table and trying to determine if there is an imbalance of high value cards (such as the tens, picture cards and aces) vs low value cards (the 2, 3, 4, 5 and 6's). At the start of a new deal whether from a single deck, double deck or multiple decks of cards, this ratio of high cards to low cards is equal to one.

To put it another way, there is an equal number of tens, picture cards and aces as there are 2 through 6's. Card counters watch the cards on the table. If on the very first round they observe a greater number of low value cards vs high value cards, then the opposite has to be true as to the ratio of these cards in the remaining deck(s) of cards to be played. As the game progresses and more cards are dealt, the ratio of high vs low value cards in the remaining deck(s) will change depending on how the cards fall. The card counter patiently waits for these imbalances to occur and when they do, he will use this knowledge to either vary the amount of money bet and/or the playing strategy.

It has been proven without a doubt through countless computer studies that deck(s) of cards that contain an excess of high value vs low value cards favors the player. At this point during the game when the remaining cards to be dealt contain an excess of tens, picture cards and aces vs 2 through 6's, the player has the advantage over the dealer on the next round of play. This is when a card counter will increase his bets from this minimum to a slightly higher bet (for example, $10 to $20). In other words, the card counter is always making larger bets when the odds shift in his favor. This is the ideal way to play blackjack if you are serious about winning.

When the opposite occurs and the remaining cards to be dealt contain an excess of low value cards, then the advantage shifts to the dealer on the next round. In this situation, the card counter will make the lowest bet or simply leave the table and play elsewhere.

The high value cards favor the player vs the dealer because unlike the dealer, the players get a bonus payoff on a blackjack. Also, players don't have to draw to a 12 through 16 hand from a ten rich deck, whereas the dealer has to draw. And when a player doubles down on 9, 10 and 11's, from a ten rich deck, he most likely will end up with a winning hand.

The low value cards favor the dealer simply because the dealer must draw on 12 through 16's. When the deck is rich in small value cards, the dealer will most likely end up with a hand that will beat the players' hands. Also, low value cards in most cases are no help for players when they double down.

If you are playing in a single or double deck game, get in the habit of watching the cards to determine if there is an excess of low vs high value cards on the table. Carry this information over from one round to the next to get an idea whether the remaining cards to be dealt are rich in high vs low value cards. Maintain a minimum bet when the remaining cards are either neutral or rich in low value cards. When the cards become rich in high value cards, then increase your bet from 1 unit to 2 units. If the cards become very rich in tens and aces, especially after half or more cards have been dealt, then increase your bet to 3 units. By betting in this manner, you will have the edge over the casino simply because you are making larger bets when you have the edge (ten rich deck) and small bets when the dealer has the edge (rich in low value cards).

If you play in multiple deck games (4, 6, 8 decks) in which the casino has a slightly greater edge vs single or double deck games, you need to learn a card counting system that assigns a point value to each card. It's not that difficult, but it does require a considerable amount of time and practice to be able to count in a casino environment.

By learning card counting, you can turn the tables on the casino and have the long term edge over them. It's a proven winning strategy to beat them at their own game.

◆ ◆ ◆

Why Do I Lose With Basic Strategy?

Casual blackjack players often ask me this question. They take the time to learn the basic blackjack playing strategy and follow the rules faithfully in the casinos, yet sometimes they end up losing. In fact, sometimes they lose on several consecutive playing sessions. Not understanding why they lose, they blame the playing strategy and revert to a more "intuitive playing strategy". If this has happened to you, perhaps this recent experience I had will clear up this anomaly.

It was about 6:00 am and I had just completed the filming of an instructional video in a Mississippi casino. The filming started at about 3:00 am and I was tired and hungry, so I decided to have breakfast in the casino's coffee shop. While eating, I couldn't help notice an empty blackjack table close to where we had just completed the video. Even though I hadn't planned on playing, something told me to go ahead and play anyway; so I did.

During the course of the next 30 minutes, I had a most

memorable playing session. No matter what I did, I won virtually every hand. I had amassed piles of chips in front of me that were stacked high like castles in the sand. I started this playing session being dealt two consecutive hands of blackjack. But this was nothing compared to what followed. I was often dealt two card hands totaling 10 and 11 and every time I doubled down, I automatically drew a ten. The few times I was dealt a pair and split, the dealer obligingly went over 21, leaving me with a big win. And every time I was dealt a lousy hand of 15 or 16 and hit, I miraculously never busted. The dealer on the other hand, was consistently dealing herself two card stiff hands (12 through 16) and had to draw. Happily, she consistently drew a big card and went over 21.

I had won more money in 30 minutes at that table than I had ever won in the same amount of time in 27 years of playing blackjack. Was this a fluke or something that sooner or later I should have expected?

The answer - it was a fluke. The same reasons that players sometimes have a losing session with basic strategy apply to why I shouldn't expect to have another spectacular 30-minute winning session in my lifetime like I had just experienced.

The reason for this has to do with what mathematicians call *variability*. If you flip a coin 100 times and bet on heads on each flip, what would you expect the outcome to be? Most likely you would say you expect heads 50 times and, likewise, tails 50 times. Seems logical. In reality, however, if you were to flip a coin 100 times and recorded the results, you most likely will end up with more or less than 50 heads (try it sometime). There is a certain natural variation from what you expect to occur. Mathematicians (don't we love them!) can actually compute with reasonable certainty what the variation from the expectation is likely to be (they call this the standard deviation). After flipping the coin 100 times, you will have a 95% chance of ending up between 40 and 60 heads. That's a spread of 20 from the expected average of 50. That is the natural variation I was talking about. And guess what? Just like flipping a coin has a variability associated with it, so does the game of blackjack.

Blackjack players must understand that this variability will sometimes cause you to lose even though you are using the optimum playing strategy. However, over many playing sessions, you will fare much better using this basic strategy than by using a seat-of-the-pants "intuitive" strategy. That's a mathematical fact that has been proven over and over again by me and others through the use of computer tests of millions of hands of blackjack and from our actual playing experiences on the tables.

Just like blackjack players shouldn't expect to win every time they play blackjack using the basic strategy, so I shouldn't expect to experience the same 30-minute spectacular winning session again. It could occur, but the probability is very low.

So, what's a blackjack player to do with this variability? The best you can do is to understand that this natural variability exists and respect it when you play blackjack. Be prepared ahead of time that this could be the night that every time you double down on an 11, you'll draw an ace (don't tell me this has never happened to you!) or every time you hit those stiff hands, out comes the picture cards. When you are having one of those playing sessions where no matter what you do, you lose hand after hand, do <u>not</u> get discouraged and abandon the basic strategy. This is not the reason you are losing. You are losing because of the variability that exists in the game.

Professional blackjack card counters understand this variability all too well and learn, sometimes the hard way, that it is a cardinal sin to overbet because the variability could cause them to go broke. From the recreational blackjack player's perspective, here are some things you can do to protect your bankroll when the cards aren't coming your way.

First, get in the habit of dividing your bankroll into several playing session bankrolls. If you find yourself losing at your first playing session, do not lose more than what you had allocated to this session. Discipline yourself to get off the table and take a break. You still have at least another session bankroll to try your skill and luck at another table. The rule to remember is to not lose it all in one session!

Second, do not overbet like the pros. Try to keep a reasonable spread between the amount you will bet and your total bankroll. It is ludicrous to make bets at a $25 minimum bet table with a bankroll of a couple hundred dollars. A few negative swings (that's another term that describes variability) and you'll soon be broke. A quick rule of thumb is to have at least 100 times your minimum bet as a bankroll.

Just like players experience variability at the blackjack tables, so do the casinos. The big difference, however, between the casinos and us, is that they have basically an unlimited bankroll to ride out the sometimes negative swings in variability that they experience (i.e. players get real lucky and win). Have you ever seen a blackjack table go broke? If players are winning and the dealer has very little chips left in the tray, what does the floor supervisor do? He simply calls for a fill and more chips are brought to the table.

What about you and me? If we overbet and lose hand after hand because of this variability, unless we are independently wealthy, we have a high risk of going broke. Moral of this story is: don't overbet!

When blackjack players start losing, they not only abandon the basic strategy but they invoke several incorrect playing habits that only cause them to lose more. This includes the following:

1. Increasing their bet size expecting the next hand will win and get them even. This is a sure way to lose your shirt. Just because you increased your bet doesn't mean your chances will improve on the next hand. If anything, you should do the opposite when you are losing: bet the minimum and if losses continue, get off the table and take a break.

2. Follow the dealer's strategy of always hitting on 16 or less and standing on 17 or more - after all the dealer is winning with this strategy. Another big mistake. Never follow the dealer strategy of hitting all hands 16 or less and standing on 17 or more. The reason is because the dealer always goes last and if you bust, your bet is lost even if the dealer subsequently busts.

3. If all else fails, blame the other players for your losses. Getting obnoxious at the table by blaming other players for making stupid playing mistakes that caused you to lose the hand is uncalled for. The fact of the matter is that the skill or lack of it by fellow players has no effect on whether or not you win or lose a hand.

The bottom line is that sooner or later, you are going to encounter a bad losing streak at the blackjack tables even though you are using the basic strategy because of the natural variability in the game. When it happens, discipline yourself to bet the minimum, change tables, change casinos and if necessary, quit for the day (the casinos will always be open the next time you want to play blackjack). Above all, do not abandon the basic strategy!

◆ ◆ ◆

Multiple Action Blackjack
Making Three Wagers Per Hand

A reader from New Jersey writes:
"I noticed several Atlantic City casinos offer a blackjack game where the players can make up to three wagers on each hand. I've never seen this game before. Can you explain how the game is played?"

The game is called *Multiple Action Blackjack*. It was

created by the Four Queens Casino in downtown Las Vegas several years ago. The game became very popular at the Four Queens and they entered into licensing agreements with casinos throughout the USA, which allows them to offer it.

In regular casino games of blackjack, you make one wager per hand. In Multiple Action Blackjack, a player can make up to three wagers per hand. It works like this.

Prior to the deal, players can make two or three wagers in separate vertical betting areas (usually circles) located in front of each player. Let's suppose you want to make the maximum of three bets. You would simply place one red casino chip in each of the three circles. You now have wagered a total of $15 prior to the dealing of the cards. The dealer will deal the cards and you would play out your hand just like you would in regular blackjack. The rules are the same. You can hit, stand, split, double, etc. Let's suppose you were dealt a 10 and 8 for an 18 and you stand. Let's also assume the dealer's upcard was an 8. After you stand, the dealer will play out his hand per normal blackjack rules. Assume the dealer drew a 9 for a total of 17 and must stand.

The net result of this hand was you won, since your 18 was higher than the dealer's 17. What now happens is that the dealer will pay you one red chip as winnings for the first red chip you wagered in the betting circle. The dealer will remove his draw card (which is the 9) and keep the original 8 upcard and your hand of 18 on the table. The dealer then draws cards to the 8 to complete a second hand. Assume the dealer drew a 2 and 10 for a 20. The dealer now compares this total with the total of your hand (remember the original 10 and 8 you were dealt is still in front of you). The dealer's 20 beats your 18 and the dealer will remove the second chip you initially wagered (meaning you lost that round). The dealer will then discard all his draw cards, keep the initial 8 upcard and your hand of 18 and again draw cards to the 8 to complete a third hand. The dealer next compares his third hand with your 18 to determine the outcome of the third bet you made.

In essence, when you play Multiple Action Blackjack, the dealer keeps the same upcard for all three hands. Depending upon what he draws for each round, your initial hand could win all three rounds, lose all three rounds or win or lose two out of three. Also, one or more rounds could end up in a tie if the dealer's hands and player's hand total are identical.

When you play Multiple Action Blackjack, you also have the option of doubling down on one, two or three of your original bets. Thus, if you wager three red chips, were dealt a 9 and 2 (total 11) and wanted to double down, you could add one additional chip next to each of the three original wagers.

Players can also split if they are dealt two like cards, but in this case, you must double all of your wagers. When the dealer's upcard is an ace, you also are allowed to make the insurance bet on 1, 2 or all 3 of your original bets.

If you make three wagers and the dealer deals you a blackjack, you would automatically win all three bets as long as the dealer's upcard is not an ace or ten value card. Each of your wagers will receive the normal 3 to 2 payoff for a winning blackjack hand. If the dealer shows an ace or 10, then the dealer must play out each hand prior to the payoff (the dealer in this case could also get blackjack, in which case the hand would tie).

The casinos are thrilled with this game because in general, their hold or average win is slightly greater than the regular game of blackjack. The main reason for this is that players are very reluctant to draw cards for fear of going over 21. If this happens, they automatically lose all three bets, therefore, they tend to stand on 12 through 16's, even when the dealer's upcard is a high value card. Making the wrong play is a big mistake that costs the player in the long run resulting in a higher casino win rate.

From a risk standpoint, you take a greater risk making three bets on one hand versus betting three simultaneous hands. Therefore, you should have a slightly greater playing bankroll than regular blackjack to keep the risk equivalent.

My advice if you want to play Multiple Action

Blackjack, is to start with only two bets (the casinos will allow two bets, but not one). Make certain you follow the correct basic playing strategy for multiple deck games. If you find yourself winning, then and only then, would I increase to three bets. But be careful...a few breaking hands could easily wipe out your profits, therefore, you need to be ready to take your profits and quit should you start losing. Or to put it another way, learn to "take the money and run!".

(Note: Some casinos now allow a single bet. In this case, bet 1 spot and as you win and want to bet more aggressively, increase to two and then three bets.)

◆ ◆ ◆

Over/Under 13 Bet

A reader from Philadelphia writes:
"I saw a strange bet on the blackjack tables in which players seem to be betting on whether their hand totals over 13 or under 13. Can you explain this bet?"

This option is a side bet that a player can make whether the total of their next two card hands will be either over 13 or under 13. Aces always count as one with this bet and the dealer always wins when the hand totals 13.

After a player makes the normal blackjack bet, he can then wager on either over 13 or under 13. A special area of the layout is available for the player to place chips on either over or under 13. A regular blackjack bet must be made in order to place an over/under 13 wager. For any given hand, the over/under 13 bet cannot be greater than the regular blackjack bet.

After the initial two cards are dealt to the player, the dealer immediately settles the over/under bets. If you wagered on the over 13, you win a 1 to 1 payoff if your initial two card hand totals 14 through 21. If the hand totals 13 or less, you lose the over bet. The same rules apply for the under 13 bet, except you win 1 to 1 if the hand totals 12 or less (you lose 13 or more).

Always keep in mind that the over/under 13 is a separate bet from the initial blackjack bet. The outcome of the over/under bet is entirely independent of the outcome on the player's hand and also of the dealer's hand. And all over/under 13 bets must be settled before the regular blackjack hand is played out.

A mathematical analysis of this bet shows that the average player who makes the over/under 13 bet will be facing a casino edge of 6.6% for the over bet and 10% for the under bet. This is a very high casino edge, which means a player's chances of consistently winning this bet are not very good. However, the odds of winning are sensitive to the composition of the cards in the shoe. This means that by keeping track of certain cards that are played, the player can predict when the over/under 13 bet becomes profitable. For example, if a player observes a lot of ten value cards vs low value cards being played, the remaining decks of cards left in the shoe are rich in low cards, which favor the under 13 bet. Special card counting systems have in fact been developed specifically for the over/under 13 bet which yield a high profit potential for the counter. However, the counting systems used for the over/under 13 bet are usually different than the counting system used for the game. Using two different counting systems at the same time is quite a formidable challenge for the average player, which is why only the serious professional players profit from the over/under 13 bet.

The bottom line is that the over/under 13 wager is not a smart bet for the average blackjack player. If you want to make this side bet, then learn a counting system designed to give you the edge.

◆ ◆ ◆

Double Exposure Blackjack

"Hey, Al, I discovered a terrific new blackjack game on my last trip to Atlantic City."

"So, what's so great about it, Sam? I play blackjack at just about every casino in town and I keep losing." "That's just the point, Al. This game is different. In fact, I think the casino managers fell asleep when they put this game on the floor."

"Now you really got me interested. What's so special about this game? I thought blackjack was blackjack."

"Well, Al, let me put it this way. Suppose you were to sit down at a blackjack table and the dealer showed you both of his cards! You heard me right, Al. You get to see with your eyes what the dealer's got before you play out your hand!"

"Oh, come on Sam, you must be joking. That would give the player too much of an advantage knowing what the dealer's hand is. Why, if I sat with a 17 and the dealer was showing a pair of picture cards (20), I'd for sure hit that 17."

"That's the point, Al. In fact, I was hitting my 17's and 18's all night and getting real lucky and drawing small cards. Even when I had a lousy hand like 15 or 16, I'd stand when I saw him with a similar hand and just watch him bust when he had to hit. Made a bundle on this game, Al. In fact, I'm planning to go tonight. Wanna come?"

This game does sound like a good deal. After all, it's every blackjack player's dream to be able to see the dealer's downcard as well as his upcard. But is it really as good as it sounds? Let's see.

The name of the game that our friends stumbled upon is called Double Exposure Blackjack. It originated in the Vegas

World Casino in Las Vegas back in 1979. Since that time, it has surfaced in casinos throughout the country under the name Show and Tell, Face Up and Peek-a-Boo Blackjack. Although the game allows the players the advantage of seeing both of the dealer's cards, the rules have been significantly modified so that the casino maintains it's edge over the players. The following table summarizes the rules for Double Exposure Blackjack and how they compare to the regular game of blackjack.

Rule	Double Exposure	Regular Blackjack
Tie Hands	Dealer wins all ties except player wins all blackjack ties	Player neither wins nor loses
Blackjack Hand	Pays even money or 1 to 1	Pays 3 to 2
Doubling	Only permitted on two card hand totaling 9,10 or 11	Player can double on any two card total
Doubling After Pair Splitting	Allowed	Allowed
Dealer Has Soft 17	Dealer must stand	Dealer must stand
Resplits	Not allowed	Allowed
Surrender	Not allowed	Some casinos allow

If you study the above rules for Double Exposure Blackjack, you'll see a bunch of negative rules that more than make up for the rule that allows you to "see" both the dealer's initial two card hand. The big negatives are dealers winning all tie hands (except blackjack ties) and the player only getting paid even money on a blackjack hand. If you crank out the mathematics (which I've done), what you'll discover is that the casino's edge for the basic strategy player in Double Exposure Blackjack is about 0.7% vs 0.3 to 0.5% for typical blackjack rules being offered in Atlantic City casinos.

A word now about the basic strategy for Double Exposure Blackjack. As you can imagine, the mathematically derived optimum playing strategy for this game is quite different than the basic strategy you would use in regular games of blackjack. When you think about it, most hands in Double Exposure Blackjack are automatic losers if you don't take the chance and hit. If you hold a 19 and the dealer shows a 19, you know you will lose (remember the dealer wins all ties) so you should hit. For those interested in learning the basic strategy for this game (and you should if you intend to play it!), I can recommend the books, *Basic Blackjack* by Stanford Wong and *Best Blackjack* by Frank Scoblete. Both contain the complete basic strategy for Double Exposure Blackjack.

◆ ◆ ◆

Live Video Blackjack

Who would have thought that one day you'd be able to walk into a casino and play blackjack without a dealer? I sure didn't think it was possible, but in fact many casinos have installed video devices that allow one or more players to play blackjack without a live dealer. These "live video blackjack" games, by Minneapolis-based Innovative Gaming Corporation, have been a big hit with players who would otherwise feel intimidated playing blackjack with a dealer and other players.

The game is a sight to behold. Arranged in a horseshoe are five or more player stations consisting of video monitors where the player cards appear and buttons that allow players to select how much they want to bet, and whether they want to hit or stand. In the middle of this horseshoe is a video screen that shows the dealer's hand. The computer in these machines can be programmed for the number of decks to be dealt and the frequency of the reshuffle. The computer shuffles the cards, deals them to each player, determines when a player busts or stands, deducts losing bets from a player's bankroll (or adds it on a winning hand), and even announces player hand totals and blackjacks, with music, of course.

On most video blackjack machines, a player can load up to $500 in credits by inserting coins in the slot or bills in the bill acceptor. You then make bets using this credit.

The minimum bet is usually $1, maximum $99. On most machines, the dealer stands on 17 through 21 (including an ace, 6 hand), and players can double down only on hard 10 or 11. Pair splitting is allowed (on some machines, resplits are allowed), but doubling after pair splitting is not. Insurance is asked whenever the dealer has an ace upcard.

Overall, the rules are not as favorable as the table game, especially if the computer is programmed for multiple decks. But the playing rules on live video blackjack machines might differ slightly from one casino to another, so check them out before you play.

Every time you make a wager, the amount is deducted from your credits. When you win a hand, you get paid 2 to 1 (you get back the one chip that was deducted when you made the bet, plus the additional winning chip).

Player blackjacks are paid at 2.5 to 1 after the initial bet is deducted from the credits. If you bet an odd amount of money and get a blackjack hand, the computer will round down (it will not pay off the 50 cents in a 2.5 to 1 payoff). Therefore, a winning tip for playing these machines is to always bet an even amount of money to get the correct 2.5 to 1 payoff (equivalent to the 1.5 to 1 payout for blackjack hands in the regular game).

The mechanics of playing electronic video blackjack are

simple. After players have indicated the amount of their bets, the computer will deal each player two upcards and show the dealer's upcard in the center console. The computer also tallies the player's hand and indicates it on the screen. Each player in turn must decide whether to stand, hit, double or split by selecting the appropriate play button in front of him. The computer shows which player's turn it is with a flashing light in front of that player. After a player makes his selection, the computer moves to the next player. The computer will allow a reasonable amount of time for a player to decide how to play his hand. However, if the player takes too long, the computer will automatically register a "stand" and move on to the next player.

Player credits are highlighted on the screen so players always know how much bankroll they have. You use your built up credits to make subsequent bets or at any time you can select the payout button and receive your credits in coins.

Of course, you should use the correct basic strategy to cut the casino's edge to as low as possible. With proper strategies, you can cut the casino's edge to about 0.5%. This means your long term loss is only 50 cents for every $100 played into these machines. Also, don't forget to insert your frequent player card. This is a good slot machine type game to rack up points on your card with a minimum expected loss.

Can these machines be beaten by skillful card counters? I gave it a try when they were first introduced in a Mississippi casino. With a single deck and a reshuffle after 40 cards, I was able to play alone against the "dealer" in late evenings and by card counting, vary my bets from $1 to $99. I was a big winner the first two out of three playing sessions. Then without warning, the machines were taken out of service and reprogrammed for four decks, with a reshuffle after every round. This completely negated the possibility of using card counting to gain an edge.

Live video blackjack games appeal to novice players who want to learn how to play blackjack for low stakes in a non-threatening environment. Besides live video blackjack, you might also see live video craps and live video roulette games at your favorite casino.

The Shuffle

Have you noticed what has happened to the simple routine of shuffling cards at the blackjack tables? In the old days, the dealer would split the 6 or 8 decks of cards into two piles. The cards from each pile would be shuffled together and before you knew it, the dealer would be handing a player the cut card. It was quick and easy.

Nowadays, casinos employ a much longer and much different shuffle. Even the undealt decks of cards left in the shoe are no longer simply placed on top of the discards. More often they are "plugged", which means they are inserted into the midst of the discards prior to shuffling. And multiple pile shuffles with criss cross intermixing of the cards followed by dilution "riffles" and card "stripping" have replaced the simple two pile shuffles.

What gives here? Are the casinos trying to impress us with these choreographed shuffles that seem to take forever to complete? Not really. It's just their way of implementing countermeasures against the new breed of skilled blackjack players known as shuffle "trackers".

Let me take you back to a playing experience I once had in an Atlantic City casino. I was holding my own in a multiple deck game, using my card counting expertise to look for favorable situations to increase my bet size. My count started to escalate indicating that the high value cards were due to come out of the shoe. I increased my bet size, but still no high cards. I was getting more anxious and excited as my count continued to climb and so did my bet size. Just when my count had reached an all time high and my advantage was sky high, that ugly looking yellow cut card came flying my way. The high cards, including a whole bunch of aces were behind the cut card in the shoe. My heart sank as I stared at that pile of beautiful high cards laying motionless in the shoe. The dealer abruptly scooped up these cards, placed them on top of the discards and started shuffling. My eyes remained focused on those cards while my mind wandered to what might have been.

To my surprise and astonishment, I was actually able to follow this clump of high cards during the dealer's shuffle. Granted, the shuffling routine was pretty simple back then, but when the dealer placed those shuffled 6 decks in front of me to cut, I knew with a fair degree of certainty that the clump of aces and high cards were about three decks from the top card. I picked up the cut card and nonchalantly placed it at about two and one half decks or just in front of where I believed those aces and high cards were located. By placing the cut card where I did, I had essentially cut the high cards and aces to the top of the pack of cards. If I was right, then those aces and ten value cards should be the first cards coming out of the next shoe. I held my breath as I made a fairly large bet at the start of the next shoe and as I had predicted, out came those beautiful cards.

What I had done (although not pre-planned) was to track a "slug" of high cards in the "cutoff deck" through the shuffle so that I was able to locate where the slug was and "cut" the favorable slug to the top of the shuffled pack. This is, in fact, what shuffle trackers can do with great accuracy which is why many casinos have resorted to the sometimes convoluted and long shuffling routines as countermeasures to shuffle trackers.

I am not by any means an expert on shuffle tracking. Although I've successfully used the technique of cutting a favorable slug of cutoffs to the top on many occasions, this is just one of many arsenals more experienced shuffle trackers use to gain the edge over the casino.

I recently met and played with a skilled shuffle tracker. This individual was able to remember where slugs of favorable (and sometimes unfavorable) cards were located in the 4 to 5 decks of cards resting in the discard tray. If there were a slug of tens that appeared during the second deck of a 6 deck shoe, this shuffle tracker would remember that the second deck from the bottom in the discard tray is rich in high cards. And with this knowledge, he was able to track those cards (or deck) through the shuffle and cut them anywhere he wanted. He could cut slugs of favorable cards to the top of the stack or cut the less favorable cards to the bottom where they would end up behind the cut card (as cutoffs for the subsequent shoe).

Not much has been written about shuffle tracking until now. It turns out casinos are keenly aware of this advanced playing technique. Many have resorted to shuffling countermeasures and are alert to players who make larger bets at the start of a new shoe.

A language has evolved that relates to shuffle tracking. The portion of cards that the dealer picks up to shuffle is known as a pick (or sometimes a garb). When the two picks are shuffled together, this is known as "riffling". And dealers have now been taught the techniques of "plugging" the cut offs and using "riffle and restack" and "stepladder" criss cross shuffling routines to more randomly mix the cards to eliminate "slugs".

What's ironic is that the shuffle trackers' betting and playing style is quite different than the conventional card counter. Card counters seek single and double deck games whereas shuffle trackers prefer multiple deck games. Card counters usually don't bet big at the start of the shoe, whereas shuffle trackers often do.

The only way to learn shuffle tracking is to buy 6 or 8 decks of cards and practice the technique at home. You need to watch and learn the specific shuffling procedure used in a casino and then recreate this shuffle at home with a slug of cutoffs. With practice, you'll be able to see for yourself where the slug will end up in the final shuffled decks of cards. As long as the dealer doesn't deviate from his shuffling routine, you really don't have to watch the shuffle in the casino! Your practice and experience tell you where those cutoff cards will be located in the final stack of shuffled cards.

Obviously, shuffle tracking is not a technique that you can learn in one evening. I've been practicing for months and still consider myself a novice. However, it is a powerful advanced strategy that when coupled with card counting can give you a decided edge over the casinos.

If you want to learn more about this technique, I can recommend Arnold Snyder's *Blackjack Forum* Newsletter. Arnold recently published an excellent series of articles in his newsletter on the theory and techniques of shuffle tracking. It is the first detailed account of this relatively new playing strategy for blackjack players.

(*Note: Since this article was written, more casinos have resorted to automatic shuffling machines as a deterrent to shuffle trackers.*)

◆ ◆ ◆

Frequently Asked Questions

Every time I am a guest on a radio or TV show, the bulk of the questions from viewers and listeners focuses on the game of blackjack. That's not too surprising considering blackjack is still the most popular table game and the only one that is beatable.

I've summarized the most often asked questions about blackjack. Perhaps the answers will help you become a more informed, successful player.

"I've been told you should always take insurance when you have a good hand, like 19 or 20. Is this the correct play?"
Too many casino players have the misconception that you should always insure a good hand. The insurance bet comes into play when the dealer's upcard is an ace. He will ask all players if they wish to make the insurance bet. In reality, the insurance bet is a side bet that you can make in which you are

betting that the dealer's unseen downcard is a ten value card (and therefore the dealer has a blackjack hand). It has nothing to do with the original bet you made or what hand you happen to be dealt (even the good hands). You are simply betting that the dealer's downcard is a ten or picture card. Unless you have some knowledge of the abundance or deficiency of the ten value cards in the decks of cards in the dealing shoe prior to the dealing of the hand (i.e. unless you are card counting), you have no business making the insurance bet. The bet has a high casino edge and should be avoided. Even if you are dealt a blackjack, you'll win 4% more money over the long haul by not taking insurance (or the equivalent even money). The bottom line is that the insurance bet is a sucker bet and should be avoided.

"Whenever there are players who don't know how to play their hands on the table, I always seem to lose. Is it true poor players affect the outcome in a negative way?"

This is another misconception amongst blackjack players. It really doesn't matter how well or for that matter how poorly your fellow players play their hands, including the player who plays last (the anchor or third base player). For every incorrect play they make that causes you to lose a hand, statistically there will be just as many times that you'll win. In essence, it will even out. However, if you get upset by the play of some nerdy players, then you should leave and play elsewhere. Don't ever play blackjack when you are emotionally upset because it could result in playing errors. Remember - playing blackjack should be a fun experience!

"I've been told to never split pairs when the dealer's upcard is a 10."

This is correct for all pairs except a pair of 8's and aces. Your optimum play is to always split aces and 8's, no matter what the dealer's upcard is. Eight's are split to break up a very poor hand of 16 (8,8). You'll lose less over the long run by splitting the 8's vs standing or hitting. Aces should always be split because you have a good chance of drawing a ten value card for 21.

"I never double down on an 11 when the dealer's upcard is a 10 because the latter is such a good card for the dealer. Is this the right play?"

No, it isn't. You'll gain an additional $6 per $100 bet when you double down vs hitting. Even though you will win less times by doubling because you give up the opportunity to draw additional cards, the fact that you get paid double your initial bet when you win accounts for the extra gain. Stick with the percentages and double on 11 vs dealer's 10.

"I never hit my 14, 15 or 16 hands when the dealer shows a 7. Is this correct?"

No, it isn't. But this does not mean you can always expect to win every hand when you hit. The bottom line is that when you are dealt a 14, 15 or 16, and the dealer's upcard is a 7, you have only two logical plays to make - hit or stand. By simulating this playing situation on a computer and playing out a million or more hands, the results show you can expect to win about 27% of the hands when you stand and about 34% when you hit. Hitting gains you 7%, but note that in either case the dealer has a greater than 50% chance of beating you. The best you can do in this losing situation is to minimize your losses by hitting.

"In the video the "ABC's of Blackjack", Telly Savalas stated it's impossible to card count when the casino uses more that two decks of cards. Is this correct?"

No, it isn't. Most casino players have the misconception that card counting involves memorizing every single card that is dealt by the dealer. That is not what card counting is all about. Counters assign a numerical value like plus one or minus one to every card. They watch all the cards on the table and then simply add or subtract the plus or minus values for every card.

The fact of the matter is that it is not more difficult to count the cards in multiple deck games than single or double deck games.

"I follow the basic playing strategy but still lose. How come?"

The basic playing strategy is a set of playing rules that defines how to play your hand depending on two factors: the hand you are dealt and the value of the dealer's upcard. The strategy is determined by computer analysis of millions of hands of blackjack. If you follow the strategy, the casino's edge is about 0.5% which means theoretically over the long term you will lose about 0.5% of all the money you bet at blackjack. However, over the short term, you could lose much more than the theoretical 0.5% or, in fact, win money. This is because of the variability that exists in the game of blackjack. But the fact remains you will always win more using the basic strategy than any other seat-of-the-pants playing strategy.

"Where is the best place to sit at the blackjack table?"

I always suggest that novice players sit toward the third base side of the table (dealer's right side). The reason is that it will give players a little extra time to decide how they should play their hand.

"Why not play the way the dealer does? After all, the casinos win money with that strategy."

The reason why casinos have the edge in the game of blackjack is because when you bust (go over 21) you automatically lose your bet even if the dealer subsequently busts. Mimicking how the dealer plays his hand is a deadly trap a lot of novice players fall into. It carries a hefty casino edge of about 5%.

◆ ◆ ◆

ᴮlackjack On ᵀhe ᴵnternet

If you have access to a computer and a Web browser (such as Netscape or Internet Explorer) then you also have access to a lot of information about the casino game of blackjack. You can read and learn about the basic playing strategies including card counting and other techniques; compute the basic strategy for any given set of playing rules or even find out what the blackjack playing rules are for *any* casino; play in a blackjack tournament on-line; read about new books on blackjack; find out which casino has the best blackjack rules; chat with other blackjack enthusiasts; post a message or question for others to read, and of course read what the experts have to say about the game.

You will find, in fact, tons of useful and informative information about blackjack on the Internet. Here is a sample of my personal favorites. Happy 'net surfing!'

http://bj21.com

Known as the Blackjack Page, this site is hosted by Stanford Wong, a well known blackjack author and publisher of *Current Blackjack News*. Here you will find one of the premier question and answer forums about blackjack posted by serious players and card counters. Anyone can post a question or discuss a question posted by someone else. There are pages dedicated to blackjack played in different regions in the USA (Las Vegas, east, midwest, south, west) and outside the USA. A typical question posted by a blackjack player from the midwest was, "Where can I find double deck games in St. Louis"? A reader posted a list of several casinos in the area that offered double deck games. The site also contains a members only Black Chip (private messages) and Green Chip (reading and posting messages) page for very serious blackjack players. The site also has a comprehensive list of other blackjack web sites that you can link to.

http://BJRnet.com

Also known as the Worldwide Blackjack Network, the site is hosted by Michael Dalton, a well known blackjack author and publisher of the *Blackjack Review Magazine*. The site contains a message board forum (similar to Wong's) where anyone can post or read messages, a chat room, an editorial page written by Dalton, and information on blackjack and poker. Since Dalton lives in Florida, you will also find an excellent message page devoted to Florida gaming. There is also a gambling archives page where you can read some good articles on blackjack (such as Dalton's 21 frequently asked questions about blackjack or articles by Michael Hall on optimal wagering, shuffle tracking, and other topics). You'll also find a diary of gaming trip reports reported by blackjack players. The site also has a good list of links to other blackjack web sites.

http://www.rge21.com

Known as the Blackjack Forum Page, the site is hosted by Arnold Snyder, well known author and publisher of blackjack books and the *Blackjack Forum Magazine*. You will find some excellent articles on blackjack written by Snyder and others. There are also a chat room, message board, blackjack playing conditions and other great stuff.

http://www. RGTonline.com

Billed as the "premier gambling 'zine' on the net", you will find good educational articles on blackjack playing and betting strategy in the gamemaster's Blackjack School page. Everything from the basic playing strategy to card counting is covered in easy to read and understand articles. There are excellent basic articles for the amateur player. This site also has lots of other information and stories about the world of casino gambling for gaming enthusiasts.

http://www.atext.com/people/skister/conds.html
Want to know what the blackjack playing rules are for a specific casino in Minnesota or for that matter any casino? This web page contains a list of blackjack playing rules for *all* casinos with the corresponding casino edge and betting limits, number of blackjack tables, number of decks and more. Hosted by Scott Kister.

http://www.conjelco.com
Click on the gamblers corner page and then click rec. gambling newsgroup. Here you will find a newsgroup dedicated to blackjack and also a summary of the most frequently asked questions about the game of blackjack. Great primer for the amateur player. The blackjack newsgroup allows individuals to share their interest in blackjack by posting and reading messages on the bulletin board.

http://www.blackjackinfo.com
Wish you could generate the correct basic strategy rules for any set of playing rules? This unique site will let you do it. Just input the playing rules and presto, it will generate the correct basic strategy. Hosted by Ken Smith.

http://lds.co.uk/tomt/index.html
This site contains an explanation of the basics of blackjack including information on basic playing strategy, learning to count, what the running count vs true count is all about, the Illustrious 18 (strategy deviations) and more. Also contains the Blackjack Puzzler. Hosted by Tom Turcich.

http://www.casinocenter.com/
Contains articles on blackjack (and other games) written by experts in the field. Also contains a data base of casinos which allows you to search for information about any casino.

Other informative web sites for blackjack players include:

http://www.casinocity.com/
Contains the best listing of casinos in the USA, what they have to offer, their addresses, number of different types of casino games available, number of restaurants, whether the casino has a hotel and if so how many rooms, other features of the casino and a handy map that shows where the casino is located.

http://home.earthlink.net/~chatterbox/gamble.html
Want to find the best hotel room deals in Vegas, Laughlin or Reno? This is the place to find it. You will also find show schedules, a listing of casino buffets and brunches, things to do in Vegas and more.

http://www.las-vegas-advisor.com
Want to find the top 10 deals in Vegas? This site contains them. Compiled and updated monthly by gaming author and publisher, Anthony Curtis.

http://www.jackpotmagazine.com
Here you will find directories for southern casinos, gaming instructions and horoscopes, feature stories on specific casinos and industry news.

(Note: Since this article was written, I've launched my own casino gambling web page at http://www.smartgaming.com. It contains articles on playing strategies for most casino games. Check it out and let me know if you like it.)

◆ ◆ ◆

Blackjack Tournament Experience

It was about 8:25 p.m. when I entered the roped off area

on the casino floor at Resorts International Casino in Atlantic City. I was looking for blackjack table #16, seat 7 which was assigned to me in the $150,000 Blackjack Tournament.

After covering the last blackjack tournament for a national gaming magazine, I decided to enter one myself and give it my best shot.

Even though I am a very good blackjack player, the format of this tournament makes it just as likely for a novice player to win as an experienced player. But the $50,000 top prize was too much to pass up.

My wife, friends and members of my Winners Circle Casino Gaming Club who had accompanied me to Resorts were disappointed that I was assigned to a blackjack table in the middle of a roped off area where they couldn't observe my play. One of the rules of the tournament is that participants are not allowed to talk to spectators which is why the 24 or so tournament tables were roped off from the spectators.

I was the last contestant to take his place on blackjack table #16. I took out five hundred dollar bills and placed them on the table. All contestants buy in for $500. The dealer gave me 2 black chips, 10 green chips and 10 red chips.

After signing some forms I was now ready to participate in my first blackjack tournament.

The tournament was being run by International Gaming Promotions (IGP East). They had a reputation for running a first class operation and from my own personal experience, I can vouch for this. Each playing round started promptly and the IGP East Staff were there observing the tables to make sure everything ran smoothly.

There were over 1500 players registered, making this the biggest Blackjack Tournament ever. The rules for the tournament were simple. Each player started with $500 in chips. Blackjack is played using normal casino rules for 55 minutes. Bets could be made from a minimum of $5 to a maximum of $500. At the end of 55 minutes, the dealer would deal five additional hands. After the last hand is completed, the player at the table with the most money (chips) is declared the winner and would advance to the next round.

I had seen enough blackjack tournaments as a spectator and columnist to realize that luck plays a big role in a relatively short 1 hour tournament. I saw players make big bets from the first hand in an effort to get a big lead and then sit back and coast. Other players bet the table minimum throughout the entire round until the last hand then bet it all and prayed.

As I anxiously fingered my pile of chips waiting for the 8:30 p.m. start, I glanced around my table looking at my opponents. Players 1 and 2 were men that I guessed were in their 50's. Player 3 had all the characteristics of a high roller. Player 4 was an elderly lady who came to the table with a shopping bag; player 5 was a meticulously dressed man from Philadelphia. Player 6 was a young man of college age and I was in seat 7, playing third base.

I had decided to card count and use a win progression for betting purposes. This means I increased my bets when I won (1-2-3-5 progression) but only if the count indicated a player favorable situation. On negative counts, I backed off my betting. This is not my normal style of betting...but then I wasn't playing my usual game of blackjack. Card counting is great for the long term advantage, but a 1 hour tournament isn't long enough for card counting to make a significant difference.

I was going to use a conservative betting spread for the first 15 minutes ($10 to $50), then get more aggressive for the next 15 minutes ($25 to $100). How I bet the last 30 minutes depended upon whether I was ahead, or behind and by how much. As I expected, the high roller in seat 3 wasted no time in getting big bucks on the table. His first bet was $50 and from then on he was the biggest bettor on the table. I had the smallest bet on the table ($5) for the first hand which I won with a 20 to the dealer's 18.

As it turned out, my opponents in seats 3, 5 and 6 were betting the most during the first 20 minutes or so and were winning more bets than they lost. At this point, I had about

$600 and they all had about $700-$800 which was fine because I was still within striking distance going into the homestretch.

Over the second 20 minutes, the high roller kept betting bigger (he was the first player at my table to start betting black, $100 chips) but his luck was changing. Within a few hands he was down to his last bet of $40 or so. If he lost he would have been out of the tournament. As it happened, he won the hand and bet and this was the start of a streak which brought him into contention right up to the last hand.

Players 1, 2 and 4 were never in contention as their luck just wasn't with them. The young college kid who had the lead with about $800 thirty minutes into the round, eventually tapped out, lost his $500 and was eliminated. The big bets by the high roller simply intimidated him into making even bigger bets. If I had his lead, I would have cooled it and tried to hold the lead as long as possible with small bets rather than continue betting big.

My story ends with the next to the last hand. I estimated the high roller and the well dressed man from Philadelphia had around $850 with the leader being a toss up. I sat with $490. They both bet first and put up modest bets of $100. I pushed out 2 black chips and prayed. I was dealt an ace and 3. Dealer showed a 6 upcard. The true count was a little less than +1. The obvious play was to double down, which I did. I pushed out my last two black chips and now had $400 on the table. A win would put me in contention for the lead going into the last hand. The two leaders stood with 17's which meant my winning the hand took on even more importance. The dealer saw my double down bet and flipped over a 4. A sigh of relief came over me as I sat comfortably with an 18 (ace, 3, 4) on a $400 bet. With the dealer showing a 6 upcard, my odds of winning the hand were good.

The final moment came when the dealer nonchalantly flipped over her downcard. It was a ten...exactly the card I had hoped for. There it was, a lovely hard 16 with the dealer having to draw a third card from a ten rich deck. She quickly drew that third card and slammed it to the table. My heart sank.

As fate had it, it was a 3 and the dealer beat me with a 19. My $400 investment was lost and for all intense purposes so was my shot at winning the table. The high roller in seat 3 who had a slight lead going into the very last hand, ended up in second place as the well dressed Philadelphia man doubled down on the last hand, won and ended up the table winner by just about $40 more than the high roller.

My wife was waiting for me outside the ropes and she could tell by the disgusted look on my face that I had bombed out. As I was telling her what happened and showing her the receipt I received for the $75 I had left (I lost $425), she calmly gave me a hug and said since she couldn't watch me play, she played a "little" blackjack and won...would you believe over $800!

(Note: I've since entered several blackjack tournaments but haven't won the big one yet. I highly recommend Stanford Wong's Tournament Blackjack Software program as a teaching aid.)

♦ ♦ ♦

Spanish 21

A local Las Vegas resident dropped me a note and asked if I knew something about a blackjack game being dealt from a deck of cards in which all the tens are removed. The name of this game is Spanish 21 and it is being offered at Bally's, Dessert Inn, Harvey's and the Riviera. Several other properties are scheduled to begin offering the new game in the next weeks.

The game is played with six decks of cards in which all the tens are removed. All other value cards include jacks, queens, kings and aces remain.

As most blackjack players know, tens are a player favorable card because you need a ten to get a blackjack hand which pays a bonus payoff of 3 to 2. By removing the tens, the casino's edge increases by about 2%. To compensate for this, Spanish 21 offers very liberal playing rules and some interesting and unique bonuses. They include the following.

1. A player gets a 3 to 2 payoff on a blackjack hand even if the dealer also has a blackjack.

2. If a player hand totals 21, it automatically wins even if the dealer also has a hand that totals 21.

3. You can split pairs including aces up to 4 times.

4. You can double down on any number of cards including after pair splitting (even splitting aces).

5. Late surrender is allowed, even after doubling down.

6. You can surrender and take insurance.

7. In addition to the 3 to 2 bonus for blackjack, Spanish 21 offers the following bonus payoffs:

5 card 21 pays 3 to 2	Any 7-7-7 pays 3 to 2
6 card 21 pays 2 to 1	7-7-7 suited pays 2 to 1
7 card 21 pays 3 to 1	7-7-7 of spades pays 3 to 1
Any 6-7-8 pays 3 to 2	7-7-7 suited with dealer showing
6-7-8 suited pays 2 to 1	any 7 upcard gets paid $1,000 for
6-7-8 of spades pays 3 to 1	$5 bet or $5,000 for $25 bet (in
	the latter case, all other betting
	players get an envy bonus of $50)

I used Wong's Blackjack Count Analyzer Software to determine the basic strategy for Spanish 21. To say the least there are many changes to basic strategy. In fact, the complete basic strategy is more complicated compared to the normal basic strategy. Even if you memorize the more complicated strategy, the casino's edge is around 0.7%. Make a few mistakes in playing strategy and that casino's edge will increase even more.

There is one booklet on the market by Lenny Frome, that analyzes the game and gives a complete basic strategy. For details, write to Lenny Frome at 5025 S. Eastern Avenue, Las Vegas, NV 89116.

(Note: Since this article was written, Spanish 21 is offered at most casinos throughout the country.)

◆ ◆ ◆

Tipping The Dealer

Why tip (or toke) a blackjack dealer? The fact of the matter is that most dealers earn minimum wage and they depend upon tips from players for their livelihood. That doesn't mean you shouldn't automatically tip a dealer every time you play. Use common sense and tip if it is warranted. If the dealer has been helpful and friendly and made your gaming experience enjoyable, a tip would be in order. But if the reverse is the case, I wouldn't bother. Not leaving a tip would hopefully send a message to the dealer that rude behavior will not go very far in this industry.

There are several ways to tip a blackjack dealer. One way is to simply put some chips on the layout and tell the dealer that the chips are for him. Most players do this at the end of their playing session. Never hand chips or cash directly to a dealer as this is not allowed in most gaming jurisdictions.

Another popular way to tip is to make a bet for the dealer on your hand. If you win your hand, the dealer bet would also win. One way to make a bet for the dealer is to place the chip(s) you are betting for him on the outside of the betting circle. The chip(s) you are betting on your hand would be in the circle and the dealer's bet would be on the outside edge. Those chips on the edge are universally understood that you are making a tip bet for the dealer on that hand.

Suppose you made a $5 bet and placed two $1 chips as a bet for the dealer. If you win the hand, the dealer would payoff your $5 bet and the $2 tip bet. It's okay to pick up your winning chips, but just leave the original $2 tip bet and the $2 payoff on the layout. When the dealer finishes collecting players losing bets and paying off the winners, he will pick up the $4 tip for himself.

Making a tip in this way does have some downside risks. In the above example, if your hand is lost to the dealer's hand, the $2 tip bet would be placed in the casino chip tray. In other words, the dealer will get nothing because your hand lost. In essence, when you win, so does the dealer. But when you lose, so does he.

I've asked many dealers whether they prefer to be given a tip outright or have the player bet it on their hand. By far the vast majority would prefer that players bet it for them on the hand in the hope they will get double the original bet as a tip. Even if their bet was lost, they appreciate the player's gesture of making a bet for them.

There is another way to make a bet for the dealer. It is less popular than the above but I have seen players tip this way. Instead of placing the chip(s) you want to bet on your hand for the dealer on the outside of the betting circle, place the chip(s) on top of your chip(s) but slightly off centered.

The difference in the two ways of betting for the dealer comes in the payoffs. When you bet on the outside of the betting circle and you win your hand, the dealer will pay you and himself. He will collect and keep the original bet you made for him plus the payoff bet. If you want to make another bet for him, you must lay out another chip. If instead you placed your tip bet on top of your chips and you win the hand, the dealer only pays you. Give him only the winning tip payoff and the original tip bet you would let ride on the next hand. In essence if you bet $5 for the dealer in this manner and you won, the dealer receives only a $5 tip and the original tip bet stays with you (to either keep or bet again for the dealer on the next hand).

I use the following rules for tipping. Use them as a guide.

1. I only tip when I am winning. If I am losing, I almost never tip.
2. If I'm betting $5 a hand, I usually tip $1. If I'm betting $10, I tip $2 and if I'm at the $25 betting level, I sometimes will make a $5 tip.
3. If the dealer is grouchy, nasty or impolite, I leave nothing.
4. I never tip more than 10-20% of my expected hourly profit as a card counter.

In some casinos, the dealer gets to keep all of the tips. However in the majority of casinos, dealers will pool their tips and share. So even though a dealer may be friendly, when you tip that money is shared amongst all the dealers. Tipping a dealer still encourages him to maintain the behavior that all blackjack players expect which is to make your game experience fun and enjoyable.

Overtipping is also something you should be careful about. I cringe every time I see a player give the dealer the extra payoff for a blackjack hand. It's tough enough to beat the casino at blackjack and when you tip the dealer you are in essence giving up a part of your profits. This is why many professional and semi-professional card counters rarely tip because the small edge they enjoy over the casino by card counting would be wiped out by dealer tipping.

Obviously, a dealer cannot affect the outcome of a hand and they are not supposed to coach players into how they should play their hand. But what they can do is help a player, especially a novice, get over the nervousness of playing blackjack for the first time by explaining the basic playing rules and table etiquette. They sometimes will even remind experienced players about an obvious double down or pair splitting opportunity they are about to miss. And if they make a mistake during the dealing of the cards, they will be quick to admit it and get the situation resolved in the player's favor. They will even sometimes give a professional player a little extra edge by placing the cut card further back into the pack of cards. A dealer, after all, is hoping you will win because they know that most players who are winning are likely to tip.

So the next time you are out for a good time, remember your dealer. Use common sense and tip just enough to show your appreciation to a dealer who is friendly and helpful. I do it because they work hard and need tips for their livelihood.

◆ ◆ ◆

Effects of Blackjack Rule Changes

Your first objective in becoming a winning blackjack player is to learn the basic blackjack playing strategy. However, the second and equally important objective is to understand the effect rule changes have on the casino's advantage. After all, it doesn't make sense to learn basic strategy and then play with unfavorable rules.

The following rules are advantageous to the player. These percentages are calculated from computer simulation studies. The higher the percentage, the more important the rule is for the player.

Early surrender	0.62%
Double down on 3 or more cards	0.21%
Six card automatic winner	0.15%
Double down after pair splitting	0.13%
Late surrender	0.05%
Resplit aces	0.05%

Now that the Casino Control Commission has started to liberalize the blackjack rules in Atlantic City, the casinos have started to offer several of the above options. For example, the Claridge, Resorts, TropWorld and Trump Plaza offer the option of doubling down after pair splitting and multiple splits. The latter was recently introduced in Atlantic City and it negated a 0.04% edge the casino had when multiple pair splitting was not allowed. Las Vegas casinos offer more of the above rules to entice players and give them a better deal.

Another important factor that a blackjack player needs to consider is the number of decks used at the table. The best game is the single-deck game, which unfortunately is not offered by any casino in Atlantic City but is readily available at other casino resorts. The more decks the casinos use, the greater their advantage over the basic strategy player for the same set of rules. The casino's advantage increases to +0.61% when eight decks are used.

The following is a rundown of the casino's advantages for blackjack with different numbers of decks:

Single deck	no advantage
Two decks	+0.35%
Four decks	+0.52%
Six decks	+0.58%
Eight decks	+0.61%

At present, only two Atlantic City casinos deal four decks-Claridge and Trump's Castle.

There are several rules that further increase the casino's advantage over the player. These rules-such as limiting a player to doubling down only on 9,10 and 11, allowing the dealer to hit a soft 17, or not allowing multiple splits-are listed with a positive percentage in the table at the end of this article. In fact, the table can be used to estimate the casino's advantage for any given set of playing rules-either in Atlantic City, Las Vegas, on Indian reservations, cruise ships or riverboats. For example, a casino that uses six decks, allows a player to double after a pair split, and offers late surrender has a +0.40% edge. This is determined by using the following figures:

Six decks	+0.58%
Double after pair splitting	-0.13%
Late surrender	-0.05%
	+0.40%

The bottom line is that to be a consistent winning blackjack player, learn basic strategy and play only those games with the most favorable playing rules.

These are the casino advantage percentages for various blackjack rules options, (positive is player unfavorable; negative is favorable).

Single deck	no advantage
Two decks	+0.35%
Four decks	+0.52%
Six decks	+0.58%
Eight decks	+0.61%
Dealer hits soft 17	+0.20%
Double on 9,10, 11 only	+0.10%
Double on 10 or 11 only	+0.20%
Resplit aces	-0.50%
Double down after splitting	-0.13%
Late surrender	-0.05%
Early surrender	-0.62%
No splitting of aces	+0.17%
Double on 3 or more cards	-0.21%
Six-card automatic winner	-0.15%
No multiple pair splitting	+0.04%

♦ ♦ ♦

3

Craps

Understanding Crap Odds

Too many crap players play the game without a clue as to the odds or probability of throwing a particular number. This doesn't imply you need a Ph.D. in math to play craps. Rather, you'll appreciate the game much better and understand the different payoffs if you become familiar with the dice probability. It's not that difficult. Read on and see what I mean.

First, the basics: Dice are six-sided cubes with the numbers 1 to 6 appearing on the faces. If you pick up a pair of dice and throw them, there are only 11 possible numbers that can be thrown. These are the numbers 2 through 12 (if you've ever seen a 13 rolled, better check the dice). What's most important to players is which of these numbers are likely to show up more than other numbers. Figuring this out is easy and the following table shows how many different combinations two dice can be thrown to achieve each number.

Number	Ways	Combinations
2	1	1-1
3	2	1-2,2-1
4	3	2-2,1-3,3-1
5	4	1-4,4-1,2-3,3-2
6	5	3-3,2-4,4-2,1-5,5-1
7	6	1-6,6-1,2-5,5-2,3-4,4-3
8	5	4-4,2-6,6-2,5-3,3-5
9	4	3-6,6-3,4-5,5-4
10	3	5-5,4-6,6-4
11	2	5-6,6-5
12	1	6-6
	36	

Notice the sum of the "ways" column totals 36. This means there are 36 different combinations of numbers that can be thrown with a pair of dice. These combinations are shown in the last column.

What do you notice about the combinations? It should be obvious that the number 7 can be rolled in more combinations (6) than any other number. Putting it another way, the 7 is the most frequent number that comes up on the dice table. How frequently? Well, the table shows that the number 7 should appear six times for every 36 dice tosses. To compute the odds of tossing a 7 is easy. If 6 out of 36 tosses gives us a 7, then 30 tosses result in another number being thrown. Therefore, the odds of rolling a 7 are 30 to 6. Or, if you divide both numbers by 6, you get 5 to 1.

Let's make sure you really understand what 5 to 1 means. Whenever you see the odds such as 5 to 1, the first number (the 5) represents the number of times that, in all likelihood, what you want to happen will not happen, compared to the second number (the 1), which represents what you want to happen. In the case of our 7, 5 to 1 means you will theoretically roll five numbers other than the 7 for every one roll of 7 (that's 5 to 1 odds).

Sometimes odds are expressed as probabilities. It's easy to convert odds to probability. Take the odds equation (5 to 1), add up both numbers, in this case 5+1=6, and then ratio the 1 (the event you want) over the total, 6 (1/6). A probability of 1/6 means the event you want (rolling a 7) will occur once out of 6 trials or rolls.

Getting back to our table, notice the symmetry of the combinations column. The 6 and 8 can be thrown in five different combinations, the 5 and 9 in four combinations and so on. The pairings make it easy to remember these "ways to make."

Let's use the chart to show how to calculate some important information for crap players. What are the odds that a player betting on pass line will win on the come-out roll? We know that a roll of 7 or 11 is an automatic winner, whereas we lose our pass-line bet if 2, 3 or 12 is thrown on the come-out roll. Check the table to calculate how many ways we can make these numbers.

Winner		Loser	
7	6 ways	2	1 way
11	2 ways	3	2 ways
		12	1 way
Total	8 ways	Total	4 ways

The pass-line bettor has 4 to 8 (or 1 to 2) odds in his favor on the come-out roll. In other words, he has a big edge on the come-out roll.

What if a 6 were thrown as a point number? What now are the odds of winning the pass-line bet? Again by checking the table you find that the 7 can be thrown six ways to five ways for the 6. The odds are 6 to 5 against us.

Crap players can also use the table to help calculate the casino's edge for any bet. You do this by comparing the true odds (from the table) to the odds payoff posted by the casino. The difference is the casino's edge. For example, bet on the hardway 4 and the casino pays you $7 if you win (7 to 1 payoff). The correct odds can be calculated from the table.

Win	Lose
2-2, 1way	3-1,1-3, plus the six combinations of 7, total 8 ways

Thus, true odds of winning a hardway 4 bet are 8 to 1, yet the casino payoff is only 7 to 1 (shortchanged $1). You calculate the casino's edge by dividing $1 by 9 (total trials) to give an 11 percent casino edge.

Study the combination table. It will help you become a more skilled, informed crap shooter.

◆ ◆ ◆

Crapapbobia

Many casino players are scared of the crap table. They'd like to play what appears to be a fun casino game but the crowd of players that usually surround a table prevents them from even watching what is going on. And even if they could see, the amount of different types of bets on the layout scares them to death. This intimidation leads to what I call crapaphobia.

Hopefully, this article will eliminate your fears from playing craps. I'll show you in a few easy steps how you can get into a game even if you've never played before.

The bet you will be making is a bet on the pass line. The next time you are in a casino, walk up to a closed crap table and take a look at the felt layout. You'll see a place on the layout with the words pass line. This is where you will be placing casino chips. Ignore everything else you see on the layout.

The first step is to purchase casino chips. Simply walk up to a crap table and in between dice throws, place your money anywhere on the layout in front of you. The dealer will pick up your cash and give it to the boxman seated in the middle of the table. He will count your cash and give the dealer the equivalent amount of casino chips. The dealer will then slide the chips in front of you. Simply bend over, pick up your chips and place them in the grooved rails that run all along the top of the table. One word of caution. Players get upset when someone dangles their hands over the railing and accidentally the dice hit the player's hands during a dice roll. So when you place your money on the table or when you pick up your chips, make sure another player isn't ready to throw the dice in your direction. If that's the case wait to put your money down or pick up your chips.

Next, glance at the top of the layout and take a look at where a black and white disc is located. If it is resting on one of the numbers at the top of the layout (numbers 4, 5, 6, 8, 9, 10), you need to wait before you place a bet on the pass line. If it rests on a number the white side of the disc is usually face up with the inscription ON. When that particular game is over, the dealer will remove the disc and flip it over so that the black side with the word OFF is faced up. He will then set it to one side. When this occurs you now place your chip on the pass line (it runs all around the table) in front of you.

One of the players will toss the dice to the opposite end of the table. This first roll is known as a come out roll. You automatically win your pass line bet if the shooter throws the numbers 7 or 11. On the other hand, if the shooter throws a 2,3 or 12, you lose your pass line bet.

A third possibility exists and that is when the shooter throws one of those numbers you see imprinted on the top of the layout (4, 5, 6, 8, 9, 10). If this occurs, the dealer will mark the number thrown by placing the disc in the ON position on the number at the top of the layout. By the way, this number is known as the shooter's point.

You still haven't won or lost you pass line bet. The bet must remain on the layout on the pass line until one of two events happens. The shooter will continue to throw the dice hoping to roll the point number again before throwing a 7. If this occurs the shooter has made his point and you will win. On the other hand, if the shooter throws a 7 before repeating the point number then all pass line bets are lost. Any other number rolled has no consequence on your pass line bet.

If you've followed me up till now you should have realized that the number 7 is a big winner for us on the come out roll but once a point number is established, the number 7 will cause us to lose.

When you win a pass line bet, the dealer will place an equivalent amount of chips next to your original chips resting on the pass line. The payoff is even money or 1 to 1. Simply pick up your winning chips and place them in the rails. When you lose, the dealer will remove your chips from the layout.

Believe it or not, that is all you need to know to play craps. The casino's edge over you when you make a pass line bet is only 1.4%. That's a lot better than playing most slot machines, roulette, the big 6 wheel, and blackjack without basic strategy. You can, in fact, reduce the casino's edge on the pass line to less than 1% by learning how to make the odds bet. But let's first walk before we run – so stick with just the pass line bet until you get comfortable playing the game.

Craps is a fun casino game where everyone shouts and roots for the shooter to make his point number. It's probably the most exciting casino game and by making the pass line bet the casino will only have a slight edge over you. With a little luck, you'll not only have fun but also the opportunity to walk away with some profits.

◆ ◆ ◆

Crap Bets.
The Good, The Bad, and The Ugly

Craps is a unique casino game because it contains some of the best and also some of the worst casino bets. It's important you know the difference if you are serious about winning.

The Good Bets

The best bets on the crap layout are the ones in which the casino's edge is 1.5% or less. Play smart and you can lower that edge to under 0.5%. The lower the casino's edge, the more money you'll win over time compared to a bet with a higher casino edge.

The best bets are: pass line and don't pass, come and don't come, the odds bet, and a place bet on the 6 and 8. The casino's edge for the basic pass line or come bet (and opposite don't pass and don't come) is 1.4%. The place bet on the 6 and 8 is 1.5%. Although we can't lower the house edge on the place bet we can lower it on the pass and come (and opposite don't pass and don't come) by making the odds bet.

Nowadays, because of fierce casino competition for crap players, casinos allow players to make an odds bet equal to double, triple, ten, twenty, even 100 times the amount of their pass line bet. The casino's edge on the latter is only about 0.021%. Folks, it just doesn't get any lower than this unless you want to learn how to card count in blackjack.

The table on the next page shows the relationship of the casino's edge with the amount of odds.

One caveat, however, if you decide to bet 10 times or higher odds. Although this will reduce the casino's edge it also will increase the amount of money you have on the layout. One roll of 7 and you'll lose the pass line and odds. Therefore, you need to have more bankroll when you start betting large amounts in odds. Or you can start off betting single odds and then when you win, keep the size of the pass line bet the same but increase your odds bet to double. Win again and increase to triple odds and so forth. This technique for getting more money on the layout during a hot roll on a bet where the casino has no advantage is explained in more detail in my book, *Craps: Take The Money and Run.*

	Casino's Edge
Pass line	1.4%
Single odds	0.8%
Double odds	0.6%
Triple odds	0.5%
5 times odds	0.3%
10 times odds	0.2%
20 times odds	0.099%
100 times odds	0.021%

The Bad Bets

These crap bets have a casino edge from 2.4 to 6.7%. Although this is not intolerable, why make bets with this high a casino edge when you can make the good bets with a lot lower casino edge?

The bad bets include (casino edge in parenthesis):

Lay 4 or 10	(2.4%)
Lay 5 or 9	(3.2%)
Place 5 or 9	(4.0%)
Lay 6 or 8	(4.0%)
Buy bets	(4.8%)
Field	(5.6%)
Place 4 or 10	(6.7%)

The Ugly Bets

Now we come to the ugly or what I also call the sucker bets of craps. Why? Because here are the bets which command a casino's edge from 9.0% up to a stratospheric 16.7%. If you like throwing your money away, here are the bets for you.

Big 6 and 8	(9.1%)
Hardway 6 or 8	(9.1%)
Hardway 4 and 10	(11.1%)
Any Craps	(11.1%)
11 or 3 proposition	(11.1%)
2 or 12 proposition	(13.9%)
Any 7	(16.7%)

You can also throw the hop bets, horn bets, world bets and insurance type bets into the category of sucker bets.

It's no secret that to be a winner in craps you must make only those bets that have a low casino edge, increase your bet size as you win consecutive bets to take advantage of a hot roll, and learn when to take the money and run. This is the basics of winning craps play and to start, make only the **best bets** on the crap table and stay away from those bad and ugly bets. It is the key to increasing your chances of winning more at the crap table.

(Note: Most recently I played craps at The Rainbow Casino in Vicksburg in which they allowed 200 times odds!)

◆ ◆ ◆

Should I Bet Right or Wrong?

Wherever crap shooters meet, the question of the advantage and disadvantage of betting right or wrong usually becomes a topic of conversation. Let's see if we can logically determine which is the better bet.

Assume Fred puts up $10 on the pass line and his buddy Sam puts $10 on don't pass. What are Fred and Sam's chances of winning on the come out roll?

We know that on the come out roll, a 7 and 11 will make Fred a big winner. And there are 6 different ways of aligning the two die to give a 7, namely 6,1; 1,6; 2,5; 5,2; 4,3; and 3,4. There are two ways to throw the 11, namely 6,5 and 5,6. Thus, Fred has a total of 8 different dice combinations that could win for him.

Sam, who has his bet on the don't pass, can only win on the come out roll if a 2 or 3 is rolled. There are three different dice combinations that will yield these numbers, namely 1,1; 1,2; and 2,1. So on the come out roll, Fred, who is betting right on the pass line has an 8 to 3 advantage of winning vs Sam, who is betting wrong or on the don't pass line.

This is a universal fact. On the come out roll in craps, the right bettor has a much better chance of winning than the wrong bettor. Right bettors automatically win if the shooter tosses those naturals (7 or 11). These numbers can be thrown in more combinations than the winning crap numbers (2 or 3) that the wrong bettors are hoping will be rolled.

This advantage, however, changes if the shooter on the come out roll throws a point number (4, 5, 6, 8, 9 or 10). If a point is established, Fred wins his pass line bet only if the shooter throws the point number again before a 7 is thrown. Since we know that 7 is the most prevalent number that appears when two dice are thrown, Fred now is at a disadvantage. A 7 will make him lose. He instead wants the point number. If the point is 4 or 10, he faces a 2 to 1 disadvantage, if the point is 5 or 9, his disadvantage is 3 to 2, and on the 6 and 8, it is 6 to 5.

Now how about Sam, our wrong bettor. Remember that his chances of winning on the come out roll were not very good. But if a point number is established, he wins if a 7 is thrown before the point repeats. And as we know, 7 is the most prevalent number, therefore once a point has been established, Sam betting wrong is favored to win over Fred, betting right.

Once again here's the difference of betting right vs wrong. On the come out, the right bettor has the advantage. Once a point is established, the advantage switches to the wrong bettor.

The question to ask is how much of the time will the right bettor have the advantage vs the wrong bettor. Based upon a mathematical analysis of the game of craps, about one third of the time a decision will be effected on the come out roll (i.e. someone will throw a 7, 11, 2 or 3). The remaining two thirds of the time, there will be a win or loss decision on a point roll. This means that one third of the time right bettors will have the advantage whereas the wrong bettor will have the advantage two thirds of the time. Psychologically it is nice to know that you have the advantage two thirds of the time which is one reason why many crap shooters bet on the wrong side or don't pass line.

Consider also the fact that most right bettors bet more than just on the pass line. Most bet on the pass line and then follow up with a few come bets, all with odds. Likewise, the wrong bettor usually has a don't pass bet with several don't come bets, all with odds.

In the situation just described, the right bettor stands to lose all his bets on just one roll of the dice (if a 7 is rolled, all of his bets are lost). On the other hand, in order for the wrong bettor to lose all of his bets, each of his numbers must repeat. One roll of the dice doesn't wipe him out. In fact, with one roll, the wrong bettor stands to win all his bets (if a 7 is rolled).

I sometimes bet wrong for the reasons cited above. I like to know I have the advantage two thirds of the time and I also like to know that one roll of the dice won't wipe me out. If the table is choppy, meaning there is no long string of numbers in between the 7's, the wrong bettor stands to win a lot of money. If a hot roll occurs, and a shooter throws lots of numbers, the wrong bettor can get wiped out in a hurry. To minimize this from occurring, I use a trick that the late craps expert, Sam Grafstein, taught me. When I bet wrong, I'll make my don't pass and don't come bets all with odds but as soon as one bet loses, I stop betting on this shooter. In this way, I'll cut my losses should the shooter end up with a hot roll.

Keep in mind that, statistically, the casino has virtually the same mathematical long term advantage over both the right vs wrong bettor. But betting wrong does have its advantages and for this reason, should be considered the next time you play craps.

◆ ◆ ◆

Removing Bets From The Crap Layout

Do you know which bets on the crap table can be taken off or removed by a player at any time and which bets cannot?

This may seem like a trivial point but you would be surprised how many players mistakenly remove or take down their bets when they in fact have the edge over the casino! You might find this hard to believe but I see it occurring on most of my casino trips.

For example, recently I observed a player make a $10 bet on the don't pass and as soon as the shooter threw eight as the point, he immediately took his bet off the layout. Of course the casino will gladly allow anyone to remove their don't pass bet once a point is established. It's not because the casino is doing us a big favor, but rather they would love to have uninformed players remove a bet from the layout in which the casino doesn't have the edge. By allowing players to do this, the casino is obviously saving money over the long run. The player on the other hand, is giving up the edge he had on his point, a luxury that doesn't happen too often in the casino.

On the other hand, once you make a pass line bet, it cannot be removed until the bet wins or loses. Consider it a contract bet – once you make it, it stays on the layout till it wins or loses. So, why this difference between removing the don't pass vs pass line bets?

On the initial role or come out throw to establish a point, the pass line bettor has the edge because he will automatically win if a 7 or 11 is tossed. These two numbers can be thrown in a total of 8 different dice combinations (for example, the 7 can be thrown by a 1,6; 6,1; 2,5; 5,2; 4,3; 3,4; or six different ways). You can only throw the 11 if the dice are aligned in either of two ways (6,5; 5,6). Add it up and you have a total of 8 (6 plus 2) ways to win on the pass line.

The pass line bettor will lose if the numbers 2, 3 or 12 are rolled on the come out roll. If you go through the same exercise as above, you'll come to the conclusion that these numbers can be rolled in 4 different dice combinations. Therefore, the pass line bettor has 8 ways to win and 4 to lose on the come out roll which means he has the edge on the come out roll. However, once a point number is established, the edge switches in the casino's favor. The reason is that the roll of 7 causes us to lose and 7 can be rolled in more different dice combinations than any point number. Because the casino has the edge once a point is established, this is the reason why they do not allow pass line bettors to remove their bet (if they did, we could all quit our jobs and become rich very quickly).

Now, how about the don't pass bettor. He was at a disadvantage on the come out roll. However, once a point is established, the edge swings to his favor since a roll of 7 will make him a winner. If you take a point of 8, the don't bettor has a 6 to 5 edge over the casino. This is why the casino will gladly allow you to remove your don't pass bet from the layout once a point is established. Doing so is one of the most ridiculous plays any gambler could make.

And finally here's a tip to make a lot of money at the crap table. If you see an uninformed player removing his don't pass bet from the layout once a point is established, ask him if you could buy the bet from him. If he has $10 on the don't pass line, give him $10 and take over his don't pass bet. You will have a 100% guarantee of showing a profit over the long run.

◆ ◆ ◆

Field of Dreams

"Hey Al, I heard you won a bundle last night at the casinos. How'd you do it?"

"You won't believe this George, but I won playing craps, a game I never played before."

"Craps! That's a pretty complicated game."

"Yea, but I found a real simple bet on the layout in which I've got the odds in my favor."

"No kidding, Al, so what's the bet?"

"It's a bet on the field. You can't miss it on the layout because the area for making the bet is big. You just have to put a dollar chip in the field betting area and if the shooter throws any of the seven numbers listed on the layout, you win a dollar. It's a one roll bet - even easier than playing the slot machines."

"But Al, how do you lose the bet?"

"Well that's the beauty of this bet, George. You see, you lose your bet only when the shooter throws any number not listed in the field. And there are only four of these losing numbers - the 5, 6, 7 and 8 - to seven winning numbers (the 2, 3, 4, 9, 10, 11 and 12). You see, I have seven chances to win and only four chances to lose. Pretty smart bet in my book!"

The logic that Al uses sounds convincing. After all there are seven winning field numbers and only four losing numbers. So on the surface it looks like a can't lose proposition.

But what Al has not considered is the frequency of rolling the winning numbers vs the losing numbers.

For every 36 times the dice are tossed it's easy to compute how many times we should expect any of the 11 possible numbers to roll. For example, we expect the 7 to appear six times out of every 36 dice rolls. The 6 and 8 should appear five times each, the 5 and 9 four times each, the 4 and 10 three times each, the 3 and 11 two times each, the 2 and 12 only once. The bottom line is that for every 36 dice throws, we should expect the winning seven field numbers to show 16 times. Sometimes they appear more frequently, sometimes less, but on average 16 times. The losing field numbers should appear 20 times out of every 36 dice throws. So if we bet a dollar on the field for 36 consecutive throws, we would expect to win $16 and lose $20 for a net loss of $4. But the casinos are generous and pay 2 to 1 on the winning 2 and 12 field numbers. This will cut our loss from $4 down to $2. The casino's edge is, therefore, the $2 we expect to lose divided by the $36 or 5.6%.

Some casinos entice players to make a field bet by paying triple odds on the 12. This means if a 12 is rolled your $1 field bet will pay $3 instead of the usual $2. This extra dollar payoff will reduce the casino's edge on field bets to 2.8%.

System hucksters also like to combine a field bet with other crap bets for a "can't lose proposition". For example, "make a bet in the field and place bet the 5, 6 and 8 and you will have every number covered except the 7!" The problem, of course, occurs when the 7 is rolled. It is the most frequently rolled number and when it shows, the players making the field and place bets will lose it all.

The bottom line is making a bet in a casino with a 3 to 5% casino edge is not smart. Even though the field bet is a popular bet because it is easy to make you are giving the casino too much of an edge. Sure you might get lucky once in a while like our friend, Al, but if you continue to make field bets the casino's edge will catch up and you will be a big loser. In fact with a casino's edge of 5%, you can expect to lose about seven times faster than the crap player who wagers on the pass line with odds.

Don't be like our friend Al. Learn to make the lower percentage crap bets instead of betting the field and your chances of walking away from the tables a winner will be significantly improved.

◆ ◆ ◆

Betting the 6 and 8

One of the popular crap bets is to wager on the 6 and 8. There are several different ways to wager on these numbers. Let's compare these ways and decide which is the best way to bet on the 6 and 8.

The first way is to make a place bet on either the 6 or 8. You should always wager $6 or multiples of $6 when making this bet since the casino pays 7 to 6 when it wins. This means you'll win $7 for the initial $6 wager (or $12 for a $10 wager and so forth). You'll win your place bet on either the 6 or 8 if the shooter throws the 6 or 8 before throwing a 7. On the other hand the bet loses if the 7 is thrown before the 6.

There are five different dice combinations that will produce the 6 and six different combinations to produce the 7. Thus, the true odds of winning the bet are 6 to 5. If the casino were to pay $6 for every $5 wagered on 6, the casino would have no edge. They create their edge by paying less than true odds, in this case 5.8 to 5 or 7 to 6. In terms of percentages the casino's edge on the 6 is 1.51% which is a fairly smart bet relative to other crap bets. (The same math holds true for the bet on the 8).

Another way to make a bet directly on the 6 or 8 is to make a buy bet. When you buy the 6 or 8, you must pay the casino a 5% commission or vigorish in return for getting a true odds payoff. The 5% commission is based upon the amount of your wager. Since one dollar is the minimum commission that most casinos charge for the buy bet, it's important that you wager at least $20 since 5% of $20 is a $1 commission. If you wagered less than $20, the casino would still charge a dollar commission and that will increase their edge dramatically.

Although you get paid $6 for every $5 wagered on the buy bet (true odds payoff), the dollar commission gives the casino a healthy 4.7% edge. You can significantly cut the casino's edge by betting $25, $30 or even $39 on the 6 or 8. The majority of casinos will still only charge a dollar commission. Therefore by increasing your bet size, you effectively reduce the casino's edge from 4.76 to about 2.5%. However, it's still not as good a bet as the place bet on the 6 or 8.

Casino dealers distinguish between place and buy bets on the 6 or 8 by placing a buy button on top of the buy wager. Some casinos, like those in Atlantic City, have a special area for placing the place bets that is different from the buy bets.

It's fair to say that the majority of smart crap players never buy the 6 or 8 but instead make the place bet. Because the casino's edge is significantly lower, the place bet is by far the better bet to make.

You can also wager on the 6 or 8 in most casinos by making a bet on the Big 6 or 8. There is a prominent area on most crap layouts to make this bet. The win/lose rules are the same as place and buy bets. You win the Big 6 or 8 if the shooter throws the 6 or 8 before the 7; you lose if the reverse happens. The problem with the Big 6 or 8 is that the casino payoff is only 1 to 1 (you don't get a 7 to 6 payoff like the place bet or 6 to 5 like the buy bet). This even odds payoff results in a whopping casino edge of 9%.

Happily for east coast crap players the Big 6 and 8 bet is not allowed in Atlantic City casinos. Other casino jurisdictions still offer this bet on their layout. Be wary and if you want to bet the 6 or 8, place these numbers and never make the Big 6 or 8 bet.

If you are a pessimist and betting against the shooter making his point, you can also bet against the 6 or 8 by making a lay bet. In essence the lay bet is the opposite of the buy bet. When you make a lay bet on 6 or 8 you must wager more to win less since the 7 has a higher probability of showing than the 6. You must also pay a 5% commission like the buy bet but in this case, the 5% is based upon the expected win. Thus a crap player would lay $24 against the 6 to win $20 and pay a dollar commission (5% of $20 is $1). The casino's edge on the lay bet (6 or 8) is 4.0%, a little too high for comfort and not a recommended best bet.

The place, buy, and lay bets can be removed from the layout by the player at any time. Just make sure in the case of the buy and lay bet that the dealer also returns the 5% commission. The place and buy bets are not live bets on the come out roll (they are not working), however the lay bet always works even on the come out roll.

The bottom line is that the best way to bet on the 6 or 8 is to make a place bet on them, always wagering in multiples of $6 for a 7 to 6 payoff. With a casino edge of only 1.5%, it's a good bet for smart crap players.

◆ ◆ ◆

Don't Pass on Craps

I spent a long holiday weekend in Atlantic City with friends and neither knew much about casino gambling except playing the slot machines. After steadily losing their money to the one arm bandits, they finally asked me if I could teach them to play one of the table games. However, they also added they didn't want to learn anything complicated and they were hoping to slow down their losses or at best break even for the rest of their weekend.

I pondered for a moment then told them to follow me to a crap table. I knew this couple enjoyed doing exciting things (how about sky diving for one) so craps would fit them fine. But I remembered their request for nothing complicated so I made it simple by teaching them how to make only one bet on the crap layout, specifically a bet on the don't pass.

I explained to them the basics of betting on the don't pass line, namely that the first roll after they make the bet will win if the shooter throws a 2 or 3. The bet would lose if instead a 7 or 11 is thrown. They quickly were able to understand that this roll was known as the come out roll and by watching the position of the indicator disc they could tell when to place their chip(s) on the layout on don't pass.

They became a little confused when I tried to explain why the casino bars the 12 on the come out roll for don't pass bettors. But at least they knew that when this happens it's sort of like a tie and their bet neither wins nor loses.

It wasn't long into my teaching session when they asked the next obvious question: "what happens if the shooter throws some number on that first throw other than the 2, 3, 7, 11, or 12"? I explained that the number thrown becomes the shooter's point and the dealer will mark that number with that indicator that looks like a hockey puck. The shooter will then continually throw the dice until one of two events occurs. If the shooter throws a 7 before throwing the number that is the point, they will win their don't pass bet and get paid even money. On the other hand, they would lose when the shooter throws the point number before the 7.

By now my friends were a little dazed by all this information but they were anxious to give it a shot. I told them to hold up a minute, I wasn't finished. They needed to determine how much to bet in relation to the amount of money they were willing to risk (their bankroll), how to set up a lock up fund with their chips, when to increase their bet, the concept of setting up quitting levels so they will not limit how much they could win and more importantly, if they got ahead would prevent them from giving back their profits to the casino (I call it taking the money and run!). I also explained the downside that if they started losing, they should take a hike, rest and try another table.

I watched them get their feet wet for the first time in their lives at a crap table at Caesars. They followed my advice and made one and only one bet on the don't pass to keep it simple. I left to play blackjack and told them to come see me when they were done playing.

As it turned out, I wasn't having much luck at the blackjack tables so I went looking for them. I found them still at the crap table and to my surprise they had quite a row of chips in the rails. In fact, they were ahead about $110 simply playing the don't pass with my money management advice. For the rest of the weekend they continued to play craps and I gradually explained to them how to lay odds along with their don't pass bet and also how to make the don't come bet with odds. By the end of the weekend, they had recouped their losses at the slot machines and had a small profit to boot. They also received a few comps for their steady play at the tables. More importantly they had learned how to play a casino game skillfully which gave them the best chance of minimizing the risk to their bankroll and with a little luck (like they had) to end up a winner. The moral of this story is you don't have to learn a complicated betting system to win at craps. That is what most players mistakenly believe. For a novice player, it's more important to keep it simple, learn good money management and have the discipline to know when to quit. These are the real keys to being a successful player.

◆ ◆ ◆

Reducing the Edge on Buy Bets

A buy bet in craps is a bet a player can make directly on one of the point numbers - 4, 5, 6, 8, 9 or 10. In essence, the player is betting that the number will repeat before the 7 appears. If this occurs the player wins the bet. If instead a 7 is rolled, the player loses the bet.

Buy bets are similar to place bets except the buy bets pay off at true odds.

Number	Place Payoff	Buy Payoff
4, 10	9 to 5	2 to 1
5, 9	7 to 5	3 to 2
6, 8	7 to 6	6 to 5

In order to get true odds payoff on a winning buy bet, a player must pay a 5% commission at the time the buy bet is made. Since the minimum value casino chip at the crap table is $1, the casinos will charge at least a $1 commission on buy bets. Therefore, if you want to make a buy bet, you should always bet at least $20 since 5% of $20 is $1. If you were to bet less than $20, the casino would still charge a $1 commission and their edge would be astronomical. Never do this!

To make a $20 buy bet on a number, you must wager $21 in chips. The dealer will put $20 on the number and the $1 commission goes to the casino bank. The dealer will also place a buy button on top of the chips to differentiate the bet from place bets.

Buy bets can be removed by the player at any time. If you ask the dealer to "take down my buy bets", make sure he returns $20 plus the $1 commission. Also it is always understood that buy bets are off or not working on the come out roll unless a player requests the contrary.

If you wager a minimum $20 on the buy bets, the casino edge compared to the similar place bets is as follows.

Number	Place Casino Edge	Buy Casino Edge
4, 10	6.67%	4.76%
5, 9	4.00%	4.76%
6, 8	1.52%	4.76%

As you can see, it's to the player's advantage to place the 5, 9, 6 and 8 and to buy the 4 and 10, since these bets have the lowest casino edge.

There is a technique however, to reduce the casino's advantage on the 5 and 9 buy bets.

Most casinos do not charge a second dollar in commission on a buy bet until the player wagers $40. Thus it costs the player the same $1 to buy a number for $35 as it does for $20.

The casino's advantage for a $20 buy bet with a $1 commission is 4.76%. A $30 buy bet with a $1 commission reduces the casino's edge to 3.23%. This is less than the 4.0% place bet on 5 and 9; therefore it pays to buy the 5 and 9 for $30 rather than to place it.

Some casinos (Atlantic City, for example), will allow a player to wager a $39 buy bet and charge only $1 commission. This reduces the casino's edge to a low 2.5%, the best buy percentage you can get. It's the smart way to buy the 5 and 9.

Use these techniques to cut the casino's edge to as low as possible and you'll be improving your chances of walking away from the tables a winner.

◆ ◆ ◆

Hedge Betting The 6 and 8

Crap playing systems are nothing more than a predetermined plan that includes where to bet and how much to bet. Often the size of the bet is dependent upon whether the previous bet won or lost.

One advantage of crap systems is that they take the subjectivity out of the game. The system tells the player "what to do" at all times and as long as you are not wagering on a high percentage bet, there is nothing wrong with following a systematic method of playing craps.

Having said all that, let's take a look at a system for making the popular place bets on the 6 and 8. I've played this system successfully over the years and although you won't win every time you use it, it will give you the opportunity to enjoy many profitable crap sessions.

To play this system, start by making a bet on the don't pass on the come out roll (assume a $10 bet). Once a point is established, make a $6 bet on the 6 and another $6 on the 8 (if either the 6 or 8 is the point, only bet $6 on the number that is not the point).

You now have 3 bets on the layout. A $10 bet on don't pass and $6 each on the 6 and 8. If the 6 or 8 is not rolled in the next three rolls, tell the dealer to remove or take down your place bets on the 6 and 8. This will leave only the don't come bet on the layout which will win if the shooter throws the 7 before throwing the point number.

If instead the shooter rolls a 6 or 8 in one of the subsequent three rolls, you will win $7 on the winning number. When this happens, tell the dealer to take down both place bets (i.e. the dealer will remove the bets from 6 and 8).

The strategy behind this betting system is to hope that the shooter throws the 6 or 8 in three dice throws. If this happens, you will immediately take down a $7 profit. If instead the shooter throws a 7 in one of the three dice throws you will lose the place bets on the 6 and 8 ($12), but win $10 on the don't pass bet (this is the hedge which cuts your net loss to $2). If the shooter doesn't throw the 6 or 8 in the next three dice throws, you take down both place bets and leave the don't pass bet. This isn't such a bad situation either since once a point is established, the don't pass bettor has the edge.

I would suggest you use a playing bankroll of at least $150 and plan to walk if you are ahead by $50 or more or you find yourself down by $50. In the latter case take a break, then try another table.

Winning $50 doesn't seem like much but if you learn to pocket those small profits it will add up over time. It's a smart way to play craps.

♦ ♦ ♦

Betting on The Come

One of the most misunderstood bets on the crap table is the come bet because the word "come" on the layout means nothing to the average player.

The come bet is a bet that has the same win and lose rules as the pass line bet except the come bet is made *after* the come out roll (first dice roll) whereas the pass line bet is made *before* the come out roll. The rules for winning the come bet are the same as the pass line bet - you are an immediate winner on the come bet if the next dice roll is 7 or 11; you lose if it's 2, 3 or 12. If a point number is rolled, that number must repeat before a 7 is rolled to win (if a 7 is rolled first, you lose).

Let's go through a few dice rolls to explain this bet in detail. Assume you've wagered $5 on the pass line and the shooter throws a 5 on the come out roll. Five now becomes the shooter's point. You win your pass line bet if the shooter throws a 5 before a 7; you lose if the opposite occurs. But before the shooter picks up the dice, you place a $5 chip in the area of the crap layout marked COME. On the next dice roll, you'll win this come bet if the dice total is 7 or 11. You lose this bet if the roll is 2, 3 or 12.

Notice that a roll of 7 on the next dice roll after you make a come bet will be a winner for your come bet, but a loser for your $5 pass line bet. This often confuses the average player, but keep in mind, every bet you make on the crap table is an independent bet, which means one bet may win or lose independent of any other bet.

Novice players are also confused as to what happens to a come bet should the next dice roll be one of the point numbers 4, 5, 6, 8, 9 or 10. Let's say you wager a $5 come bet and the next dice roll is a 6. Six has now become your come point. The dealer will pick up your $5 bet in the area marked COME and place your bet inside the 6 point box. You win this $5 bet if the shooter repeats your come point 6 before throwing a 7. You lose if a 7 is rolled before a 6.

Players are not limited to making only one come bet. In fact a come bet can be made before every dice roll, except as I mentioned previously, the initial come out roll (which is when you wager on the pass line). Bear in mind, each come bet can win or lose independently of the other come bets.

Making several come bets is smart because it allows you to take advantage of a "hot roll," where point numbers are repeating without the appearance of the 7. If you have come bets on several point numbers, you will be in a good position to capitalize on hot rolls.

Remember that once you establish a come point number, it will lose if a 7 is rolled before the number. So if you have a come bet on the come points 4, 5, or 6, for example, and the shooter throws a 7, you lose all your bets. To minimize this catastrophe and still be in a position to capitalize on the hot roll, I recommend making a maximum of two come bets in addition to the initial pass line bet.

The house advantage on the come bet is 1.4%. This puts it in the category of a "smart bet" for the player. You can lower this advantage even more by learning how to make an odds bet along with your come bet.

If you wager $5 in the COME area and the shooter throws a 4, the dealer will move your $5 chip to the 4 point box. To make the odds bet, you simply place another $5 chip in the COME area, get the dealer's attention and say loud and clear "put odds on that 4." The dealer will pick up your $5 chip and place it slightly off center on top of your $5 chip resting in the 4 point box. You now have two $5 chips "on the 4." If the 4 is rolled before a 7, your bet wins. The bottom $5 chip will win $5. The top $5 chip (odds bet) will win, in the case of the point number 4, a total of $10.

The odds bet is paid off differently for each of the come point numbers. For the 4 and 10, the odds payoff is 2-to-1; on the 5 and 9, it's 3-to-2; and the 6 and 8 odds bet pays 6-to-5. By making a single odds bet on all your come point numbers, you will reduce the house percent to a low 0.8%. Other than playing blackjack skillfully, a come bet with odds is one of the very best bets in the casino.

When you win a come bet the dealer will put your winnings in the COME area (where you initially made the bet). It's your responsibility to pick up your chips. If you don't, then the chips will ride as a new come bet for the next dice roll.

Also, once a come bet is made, it cannot be removed from the layout by a player. The bet must remain on the layout until it either wins or loses. The odds portion of the come bet, however, may be removed by a player at any time (though a smart player should never do this).

In the event a player has a come bet with odds on a come point number, it is understood that the odds are off on the come out or first roll. If you want to have the odds bet working, you must state this to the dealer prior to the come out roll by saying "keep my odds on the 8 working." The dealer will acknowledge this by putting an ON button on top of your odds bet.

Come betting was designed by the casino to permit continual betting on every dice roll by the right bettor. The more money bet, the greater is the casino's profit potential since percentages are working in the casino's favor on every bet.

But by making come bets with odds you will be giving the casino little in the way of an advantage, and with a little luck, you will be able to capitalize on those "hot rolls."

◆ ◆ ◆

100-Times Odds ~ A Good Deal or Not?

More and more casinos are implementing the option that

allows crap players to bet up to 100-times the multiple of their pass line bet (ditto for don't pass, come, and don't come). The casino's edge can be significantly reduced by taking 100-times odds to only 0.021%, or an expected loss of 2 cents per hundred dollars wagered. Although this looks like a terrific deal, what the casinos don't tell you is that your expected loss remains the same whether or not you take the 100-times odds or just bet the pass line with no odds. How can this be? Because the 0.021% casino edge is based on the total the player wagers on the pass line and odds. The 100-times odds just forces a player to bet more. The expected loss for a player betting $10 on the pass line will be the same whether he takes no odds, double odds, triple odds, or even 100-times odds. That loss is 1.4% times the $10 or $1.40.

So what are the advantages of 100-times odds? Certainly if you are a high roller that normally bets a black chip on the pass line, you need to rethink your playing strategy. Your expected loss for that $100 bet is $1.40. By playing in a casino that allows a dollar minimum with 100-times odds, you can have the same amount of action riding on the line by betting a dollar on pass line then taking $100 in odds. Your expected loss is reduced from the $1.40 to only 2 cents. That's a big difference.

If you are an average player betting $5 or $10 on the pass line, be careful about getting carried away and putting 100-times that on odds. You will have a lot of money riding on the table at one time and a few consecutive losing rolls could put a big dent in your bankroll (remember that when the pass line bet loses, so does the odds). If you don't have the fortitude or bankroll to bet 100-times odds, try this technique. Start your odds betting level at single or double odds and then when you start winning consecutive pass line bets, increase the amount you bet on the odds to a higher level. This technique of increasing your bets on a wager where the casino has no edge (the odds) is discussed in more detail in my book, *Craps: Take The Money and Run*.

Another advantage of 100-times odds is that mathematically a gambler has a higher probability of achieving a win goal, like doubling his bankroll, before losing it all. For example, a player with a 10,000 unit bankroll betting an average of 70 betting units on the pass line without odds has only a 1.7% chance of doubling the bankroll before losing it. Another player betting the same average 70 betting units, but on the pass line with 100-times odds, has a significantly higher (49%) chance of doubling it before losing it. Big bettors who take advantage of 100-times odds and get lucky can wreak havoc on a casino's bottom line because they have a higher probability of achieving some gain. If they are smart, when they achieve that gain they should quit playing. If instead they get greedy and continue to play to win even more, the mathematics of a negative expectation game (even with 100-times odds the casino still has the edge!) will kick in and a player will eventually lose his profit and then some. Moral: when ahead, discipline yourself to "take the money (profits) and run to the nearest exit".

♦ ♦ ♦

Taking Advantage of a Hot Roll

It was late at night when the young man strolled up to the crap table. Up till now the table had been ice cold and everyone was losing their shirt. However, all eyes now focused on this newcomer as the dealer pushed the dice in front of him. The young man put $3 on the pass line, picked up the pair of dice, and flung them to the far end of the table. *"Yoleven"* announced the dealer, *"pay the front line"*.

All the player's frowns turned into smiles as the dealers at last started to pay off. The dealer announced *"the same shooter is coming out"* as the players finished making their next round of bets. The young man put three white chips on the pass line, picked up the dice and flung them down the table. One die came to rest with a 6 showing, the other rebounded against the padding, spun around for what seemed like eternity, then came to rest with the five showing. *"Yoleven, pay the front line"* yelled the dealer. Suddenly, the players knew that something good was going to happen with this young shooter.

Players who had been betting white ($1) chips were now betting reds ($5) and the red chip players were betting greens ($25). The young shooter again bet $3 on the pass line, flung the dice, and this time the table seemed to jump about 10 feet as the dealer roared, *"Another Yoleven, pay the front line"*. Players were cheering wildly as the dealers were paying everyone off. All the screaming and yelling at the table could be heard throughout the casino.

There was no doubt in the player's minds that this could be the start of that monster roll all crap players dream about. As they were feverishly piling chips on the layout, curious onlookers who heard the commotion tried to squeeze their way around the table and make bets before the next dice roll.

The dealer pushed the dice with his stick to the young man. True to form the young shooter again made his $3 bet on the pass line, picked up the dice, and to the screams of veteran players shouting "hands up", threw them to the other end of the table. *"Winner seven, take the don't pass and pay the pass line"* yelled the stickman as bedlam rained at the table. The players were cheering and screaming with delight as the boxmen were passing piles of chips to the dealers to pay off all the winning bets.

All the excitement brought the pit boss to the table who wasn't happy with what he saw. Several players were now betting black ($100) chips, some even wagered $500 on the pass line, the table maximum. Markers were being written as fast as they could handle all the action. The boss called for more chips to be brought to the table. He also called for a crew change in the hopes this would bring bad luck to the shooter. But it didn't.

In the course of the next 15 minutes, this youngster held

those dice and threw nothing but point number after point number. The number 7 was nowhere to be seen or heard. He continued wagering $3 on the pass line and after a point number was established made a maximum of two additional $3 come bets. Players betting against the young shooter were getting creamed. Players betting with the youngster were winning and pressing or increasing their bets. The dealers were paying off hundreds, even thousands of dollars to them. They in turn were tipping the dealers after every winning coup. Everyone was happy, except the pit boss. It was his worst nightmare watching the dealers pay off thousands of dollars of the casino bank to these lucky players. But all he could do was watch and sweat as the youngster kept rolling those numbers.

Finally after 15 minutes of a monster roll, the young shooter sevened out. The pit boss breathed a sigh of relief, but the damage was already done as the casino lost an estimated twenty thousand dollars in a short 15 minutes. The youngster who made it all happen with his hot roll was given a round of applause by his fellow players. Several tossed him a few red and green chips as a gesture of appreciation for his excellent roll.

As the dice were passed to the next shooter, the youngster nervously slid his piles of chips to the dealer and asked to "color up". He walked away from the table with a black chip ($100) and a few green chips. His heart still pounding, he couldn't wait to tell his wife how much he had won playing craps. All of a sudden, he felt a tap on his shoulder. He turned and staring him in the face was the very same pit boss who had just sweat through his monster roll. "Young man," he said, "if you knew how to play craps, you could have just won a couple thousand bucks." He walked away saying nothing else. The young shooter was perplexed by his comment and didn't fully understand what the pit boss was trying to tell him. But who cared anyway, as he clutched onto his winning chips anxiously looking for his wife to share the good news of his winnings.

How do I know the facts of this story so well? I was that young shooter and this was one of my first learning experiences at the crap tables. It wasn't until several years later after I studied and learned more about the game, that I finally comprehended what the pit boss was trying to tell me that night. He was right - I could have won thousands on my monster roll if only I would have increased my bets as I was making point after point.

Most knowledgeable crap players understand that it is possible to win a lot of money in a short period of time playing craps if you take advantage of a hot roll if and when it occurs by increasing your bets. However, this strategy has a certain amount of risk depending on what bets you make on the layout, and how aggressive you increase your betting level.

First, do not, I repeat, do not increase your bets following a losing decision. Desperate crap players take this approach in the hopes that the next dice toss will be a winner and get them even. It's a losing strategy from the word go. When you lose, you should cut back on the amount of your next bet and hope that your luck changes. If necessary, get off the table and try your luck at another table. If you still find yourself in a losing posture, it's best to call it quits for the night. But please don't throw good money after bad by pressing your bets to get even.

The secret to winning money at craps is to be ready to take full advantage of a hot roll when it happens. Notice, I said "when it happens". Most of the time when you play craps, you'll be spinning your wheels patiently waiting for someone to throw lots of numbers and making lots of points. This is the time you want to strike by gradually increasing the size of your bets as you win consecutive dice decisions. Notice I said gradually. I don't believe nor am I impressed with players who constantly tell the dealer to press or double their bets after every win. The problem with this strategy is all the player's profits are on the layout instead of in the rails. One toss of 7 on a point roll and poof, the profits will disappear faster than you can say abracadabra.

Seasoned crap players will increase their bets on the pass line. A simple betting strategy is to just increase the amount of your pass line bet by about 50%. The betting progression is: $5, $8, $10, $15, $25, $40, etc. When a bet is lost, start the progression over with the minimum bet. If you are lucky enough to win a few bets in a row, you'll show a profit for the progression even though you lost the last bet. If instead, you happen to be on the right table at the right time when a monster roll occurs, you'll win big with this betting progression.

But nowadays, there is an even better way to get more money on the table when a shooter gets hot. Instead of increasing your bets on the pass line, why not instead increase your bets on the odds?

In the past, casinos limited the amount of money a player could wager on odds to a multiple of 2 to 3 times the amount wagered on the pass line. Thus double and triple odds crap tables were more or less the norm. In their attempt to attract more players to their crap tables, casinos began to increase the amount they would allow players to wager on odds. Triple odds quickly went to 5, 10 even 20-times odds. Last year, history was made when several casinos around the country implemented the unheard of 100-times odds. And recently I played craps at the Rainbow Casino in Vicksburg, MS with 200-times odds!

These higher limits on the odds bet gives astute crap players a chance to lower their cost per roll while still getting more money on the table during a hot roll. Here is how it works.

First, bet as small as the casino will allow on the pass line. At the Rainbow Casino, for example, I was betting the table minimum of $2 on the pass line. Once a point is established, bet either single or double odds. If the shooter makes his point and you win your pass line and odds bet, make another $2 wager on the pass line and increase your odds bet by about 50%. As long as the shooter keeps making his point, you keep incrementally increasing the amount you wager on the odds up to the maximum allowed if you wish.

If you follow this strategy of keeping your pass line bet at the table minimum on each roll and increase the amount of the odds bet by about 50% after every win, it would take only 2 winning rolls (followed by a loss) to show a small profit. If you get lucky and win 4, 5, 6 or more bets in a row before the shooter sevens out the profits begin to escalate. For example, if you bet a minimum $2 on the pass line and win 5 in a row then lose, you'll be ahead about $60 for the progression. Win 7 in a row (that's a real hot shooter), and you'll be ahead about $150. Get real lucky and win 2 more (total 9 in a row) and now you'll be showing a handsome profit of about $450.

The real beauty of using the odds bet to increase your betting level comes when you start to calculate your cost per roll. Since the odds bet has no casino advantage, your cost per roll is simply the amount wagered on the pass line times the 1.4% casino edge on the pass line. In our example, a $2 pass line bet would cost 3 cents. It will cost the same 3 cents whether you bet $2 on the pass line with $10 odds, or $20 odds, or for that matter $400 in odds. In other words, you can increase the amount of money you have on the layout when a shooter gets hot using the odds bet *without increasing your cost*.

To take advantage of this betting strategy, always keep your pass line bet as low as possible. Most casinos that offer 100 and 200-times odds will allow a pass line bet as low as $1, $2 or $3 (some however require a $5 minimum). The best deal is a $1 minimum since your cost per roll would only be one and a half cents no matter how large you bet on odds.

If you are normally a green ($25) or black ($100) chip player, you can still take advantage of this betting strategy. Instead of betting $25 on the pass line, bet instead $1 and then start your odds betting level at $25. You'll have the same amount of money on the layout but with a lower cost per roll (a penny and a half vs 35 cents). Increase the odds bet by 50%

following each winning roll and more often than not, you'll still have profits in the rails and in your pockets once the shooter sevens out.

As you can see this method of betting is amenable to low rollers and high rollers. If you have a limited bankroll, it's best to start your odds betting at the single or double odds level. For larger bankrolls, start your odds betting level at a higher odds multiple. Just remember to keep the amount of your pass line bet at the table minimum.

This betting technique can also be used for come bets. I normally make 2 come bets with odds along with my pass line bet. As each independent bet wins, I increase my odds betting level appropriately. By having three bets on the layout, profits will dramatically escalate if a shooter holds the dice and throws nothing but point numbers while you incrementally increase your odds bet on all three bets by 50%.

Of course this betting technique will only work if a shooter gets hot and makes several passes in a row. If the dice are passing from one shooter to the next because no one is consistently making their point number, then don't expect to win any money with this betting technique. Your goal is bankroll preservation while you patiently wait for someone to get hot. When and if it happens, you'll be ready to take full advantage of your good fortune. If it doesn't happen, you'll be no more worse off than anyone else betting the pass line.

The lesson to be learned, like the one I learned some 27 years ago, is that to win serious money on the crap tables you need to incrementally increase your bets following consecutive wins. By taking advantage of the high multiple odds as a way to get more money on the layout, you will be able to achieve this goal at minimum cost. Follow this strategy and if lady luck blesses you with that monster roll, then please make the next smart move and take your profits and run! It's the smart way to play craps.

◆ ◆ ◆

Predicting The Next Dice Roll

A reader sent me this question.

"Is it possible to calculate the odds of crap numbers rolling back to back? In other words, what would be the odds of rolling a 4, then having another 4 roll a second time. What would be the odds of a 5 (or 6) rolling back to back? Or how about a 4, 5, or 6 rolling three times in succession?

"What would be the odds of predicting or calling the next number before the dice roll? For example prior to the come out roll, I buy the 4 because I feel as if the 4 will roll and tell the dealer my buy bet is working on the come out roll. Now you tell me, what are the odds of a 4 actually rolling? What would be the odds of calling a 5 or 6 before the dice roll and the number predicted is thrown?

"Do you know of anyone who has developed a system or method to help crap players predict the next number to be rolled?"

First let me answer the question of what are the odds of rolling any crap number in succession.

To calculate this you need to refer to the following table which lists the probability of rolling any number in craps.

NUMBER	PROBABILITY
2 or 12	1/36
3 or 11	2/36
4 or 10	3/36
5 or 9	4/36
6 or 8	5/36
7	6/36

What the above table tells us is that the probability of throwing a 4 is 3/36 which if you round is 1/12. In other words, you have 1 chance in 12 of picking up a pair of dice and throwing a 4.

Now how about the probability of throwing a 4 followed by another 4? Calculating the probability of this happening is easy. It is simply the multiplication of the probability of throwing the first 4 times the probability of throwing it again or 3/36 times 3/36 equals 9/1296. If you round, you end up with the probability of throwing a 4 followed by another 4 is 1 in 144.

You can use the same arithmetic to calculate the probability of throwing any crap number any number of times in a row. The results of these calculations for the 4, 5 and 6 thrown two or three times in a row are summarized below.

NUMBER	PROBABILITY TWO TIMES IN A ROW	PROBABILITY THREE TIMES IN A ROW
4	1/144	1/1728
5	1/81	1/729
6	1/52	1/373

Please note that I have taken the liberty of rounding some of the above numbers so that they do not become unwieldy.

Notice that the probability of throwing three 4's in a row is 1 in 1,728. This is the same as saying the odds of throwing three 4's in a row is 1,727 to 1. Which is why you don't see too many 4's thrown in succession on the crap table.

The last part of the reader's question has to do with predicting what number will be rolled prior to the throw of the dice. Unfortunately the dice do not have a memory and couldn't care less what numbers were thrown in the past. Each dice throw is an independent event. Therefore with an honest pair of dice and a complete random roll of the dice, it is impossible to predict what number will be thrown. If it were otherwise, the casinos would be losing a bundle and the game of craps as we know it would cease to be offered in casinos.

The best you can do as a crap player is to make only bets that have the lowest casino advantage, learn to increase your bets when you are winning (not losing), and discipline yourself to take the money (profits) and run!

◆ ◆ ◆

Bocce Dice

It was a crowded and noisy crap table when I squeezed in to play. It was obvious the table was hot as chips were piled high on the layout and the players were screaming with every dice throw. How hot you ask? The next three dice throws were all hard sixes!

I started my betting with a bet on the pass line. After a point was established I made the odds bet. I also made two more come bets with odds. Following the strategy in my book, *Craps: Take The Money & Run*, whenever the player made a point or come number I increased my odds bet (keeping the pass and come bet the same). After I was ahead I also placed the 6 or 8 if they weren't covered by a pass or come bet.

In the course of the next half hour, every bet I made was a winner. I kept progressing my odds bet up to the maximum ten times then started to progress my basic pass line bet. The winning chips were filling the rails. It was a good feeling.

Then all of a sudden something happened which I had never seen in my 26 years of playing craps. The point was 6 and the shooter threw the dice toward the other end of the table. One die rebounded off the back wall and came to rest with the number 3 pointing up. The other die literally flew into the dice bowl then suddenly one die from the bowl came meekly dribbling across the layout and came to rest. A 3 was showing but before the stickman could announce that 6 was rolled hard and a winner for the pass line, the boxman roared "no roll".

Within a split second all the players were screaming at the boxman for his call. He tried to explain to the players that it was a no roll because the die that flew into the dice bowl was not the same die that came out (sort of like the Italian game of bocce). The players contend it was the same die. In fact everything happened so fast no one really knew what die came out of the bowl.

To say the least the players were starting to get hot under the collar since many of them had hundreds riding on that call. Fortunately I spotted the shift supervisor and motioned him over. After listening to the boxman and the players' story, he reversed the boxman's call and told the dealers to pay off.

I estimate it cost the casino a few grand for making that call. But the casino (which happened to be the Grand in Mississippi) certainly won my respect for giving the players the benefit of the doubt. It's a smart way of doing business and generating player loyalty.

◆ ◆ ◆

Proposition Betting

Intelligent gamblers know which bets in the casino will give them the best return for their investment. They seek out the bets with the lowest house percentage knowing that these bets will increase their chances of leaving with some of the casino's money. But intelligent gamblers also know which bets to avoid like the plague-the ones where the house percentage or advantage makes winning a rare occurrence. Let's explore a few of these awful bets and perhaps try to logically deduce why gamblers make them.

"Four hard four, points four!" "OK, who wants the "yo-leven?" "Ten dollars on any craps!" The typical jargon of the "stickperson" at the crap table. His primary job is to control the pace of the game and also to entice players into making the high-percentage proposition bets.

There are two kinds of proposition bets in craps: the "hardway" bets and the "one-roll" bets. The location for making the majority of these bets is right in the middle of the layout; this is why the stickman is responsible for handling these bets.

There are four hardway bets that a player can make. There's a bet on the hardway 4, 6, 8 or 10. If a player makes a bet on the hardway 4, for example, he's betting that the shooter or dice thrower will eventually toss the number 4 in the exact combination of 2, 2. This is known as the hard 4. A 4 thrown easy would be 1, 3 or 3, 1. Thus a bettor prays that the number 4 is thrown hard (2, 2) before the number is thrown easy (1, 3 or 3, 1) or before a 7 is thrown. If it does, he wins. If instead the 4 is thrown easy or a 7 is rolled, he loses.

To make this bet, a player must put his money on the layout and announce the bet "five dollars on hard four" to the stickperson.

The payoff on a winning hardway bet is 9-to-1 for hard 6 and 8; and 7-to-1 on hard 4 and 10. Mathematically, the house advantage is 9.1% and 11.1%, respectively, horrendous when you consider a pass-line bet has only a 1.4% house advantage.

Typical one-roll proposition bets include a bet on any 7, any craps, 2, 12, 3, and 11.

Here a player makes a bet that is good for only one dice roll. For example, a player who wagers "five dollars on the yo" is betting that the very next dice roll will produce the 11 ("ee-ooo-leven"). If it does he wins; if it doesn't he automatically loses. In Atlantic City, two of the more popular one-roll bets are the C-E and horn bets. The C-E bet is a wager that either craps (2, 3 or 12) or 11 will be rolled on the next dice toss. Small C and E circles on the layout are used by the stickperson to position the bet. The C-E betting area also has arrows pointing in the direction of the bettor who made the bet so the dealer can easily determine who belongs to each bet. The horn bet covers the numbers 2, 12, 3 and 11. The bet on the horn must be made in multiples of four chips. If one of the numbers appears on the dice toss, one of the chips is paid off at the prevailing odds payoff for the winning bet and the remaining three chips are lost to the house.

One more peculiarity about proposition bets is that if you make a proposition bet and win, the dealer will only give you your winnings, and the original bet is left on the layout. It's an automatic repeat wager and the stickperson will announce, "And you're up again to win, sir." A player has the option to remove the wager and does so by announcing to the dealer, "Down with my bet."

Proposition bets and hardways have a house percentage anywhere from 9.1% to a whopping 16.6%. By anyone's recommendation, including mine, they should be avoided at all costs. Yet, if you wander past a crap table or get into a game, you'll see players constantly making these bets. Why? For one, people around the table enjoy tossing their chips to the stickperson and directing him to bet the craps, hardways, 11, etc. Usually when a player is caught up in the excitement and feeling lucky or when he is trying to impress someone or simply doesn't know any better, these bets are very tempting. And the thought of making a quick killing with those high payoffs afforded by the proposition bets or perhaps to use the proposition bet to ensure a pass-line or don't-pass bet are more reasons that players make them. The bottom line is simply this: If you continue to make these bets for any of the above reasons, there is absolutely no way you can expect to be a consistent winner at craps.

(Note: The horn high bet is similar to a horn bet except the player wagers in $5 multiples and designates which number, the higher number, has $2 riding on it. The hop bet is a one roll wager on any number that is not otherwise offered on the layout as a one roll wager-such as a one roll wager on number 9.)

◆ ◆ ◆

Live Video Craps

Live video craps allow up to 6 players to play craps without a dealer. The game is played on a rectangular table which contains a video screen that simulates the crap layout. The layout is different than the normal crap layout since you can't make don't pass and don't come bets. Bets allowed include pass line, come, field bets, place bets on all the numbers from 2 thru 12 (except 7), hardway bets on 4, 6, 8, 10 and the proposition bets on the 2, 3, 11 and 12. Only single odds are allowed on pass line and come bets.

In this game, pass line bettors win if 7 is rolled on the come out roll. Any other number tossed becomes the shooters point (including 2, 3, 12 and 11). Players use a trackball to place an arrow on the layout where they want to wager and then push a button to indicate the size of the bet. The computer will wait about 20 seconds to allow players to make bets, then announce for one player to roll the dice by spinning the trackball. When the latter is done a pair of dice will fly across the screen, bounce off the sides with sound effects and then come to rest. The computer will announce the number rolled then automatically pay off the winning bets, collect losing bets (with a simulated rake that sweeps the losing bets from the table!) then announce to the players to make their bets for the next roll.

Players can insert up to $40 in credits prior to making bets. As the players make bets, the amount of the bet is deducted from their credit. When they win a bet, it's added to their credit. A credit meter at each player's station keeps track of each player's bankroll. At any time a player can cash out.

You must bet the pass line if you want to roll the dice. Even though the computer allows a certain time for players to make their bets, you need to be fairly quick in positioning your bets with the trackball because the computer gives no advanced notice of "no more bets".

The payoffs listed on the table for the various hardways and proposition bets are listed as "for" rather than "to". What this means is that on the standard table the payoff for a winning hardway 6 bet is 9 to 1 or 9-1. Your initial one chip wins you nine more chips. On the electronic version, the payoff for the same bet is listed as 10 for 1. This means you win 10 chips but the computer keeps the initial one chip wager. Your net win is still 9 chips. In other words, 9 to 1 is the same as 10 for 1.

A quick analysis of several of the listed payoffs on this video game shows worse odds in some cases than the standard game. For example, a bet on 2 or 12 on a standard table pays off at 30 to 1. On the video version you get paid 30 for 1 or 29 to 1. Ditto for the bets on 3 or 11; 14 to 1 vs 15 to 1. The rest of the bets pay very close or equal to the payouts on the standard table.

The problem with the rules on video craps is not winning when an 11 is thrown on a come out roll. The overall casino edge on the pass line is around 5.4%, considerably more than the 1.4% you can get in the standard game.

It's fun to watch these video marvels with neat graphics and sound effects. A computer simulated voice even announces each number rolled. It's also a good learning tool for the beginner to get his feet wet in the basics of craps at a relatively low cost per roll. But once you've learned the basics of how to play, I'd suggest moving up to the big tables where the odds are better.

◆ ◆ ◆

Converted Come bet

I once attended a mini lecture by the late Sam Grafstein who knew more about the game of craps than anyone I had ever met. We played together in Atlantic City and he taught me a lot about the game. This particular evening he was addressing a group of high rollers about the come vs place bets. I will take the liberty of paraphrasing what Sam was teaching them that night about what he called the converted come bet.

"OK crap shooters, who can tell me in 25 words or less what are the advantages of come betting and place betting. I know you place bettors always tout placing numbers as the better bet. After all, the number only has to repeat once for a win whereas a come bettor's number must be rolled twice. Also the place bettor can manipulate his bets any damn way he wants. He can leave it on or take it down. The come bet - well, the bet must remain on the layout until it wins or loses which leaves the come bettor no flexibility. In the other corner is the come bettor who poo poo's all this and points to that one undeniable statistical fact of life that the house advantage is less on the come bet with odds than with the place bet.

"Well, ladies and gentlemen, I have a compromise bet that I've developed for the Bahamas Craps game where come bets are not allowed. I call it the converted come bet and you can use it anywhere craps is played.

"Here's how it works. Instead of making a bet on the come line, wait for the shooter to roll a point and then make a place bet on the number just rolled. Now the number only needs to be rolled once for us to win at place bet payoff odds".

Sam's converted come bet is, in fact, a nice compromise for those bettors who want the flexibility of a place bet. Just wait for a number to be rolled first then place that number. In the case of a 4 or 10, Sam preached to buy the number rather than place it to get a lower house vig. For the 5, 6, 8, 9 just place it after it is rolled.

Sam taught a strategy of starting with a pass line bet followed by two converted come bets. Then stop betting. As bets won he would preach a 50% betting progression and keep the left over chips from the win (profits) in a lock up fund.

I was fortunate to have met and played with Sam. He

influenced me more than anyone else when it comes to playing craps. He was quite a character who loved the game and loved to teach it to players. If you want to learn more about the converted come bet, I highly recommend you consult one of Sam's books on craps.

♦ ♦ ♦

Money Management At Craps

The one danger in playing craps is not knowing at any given time how much you are ahead or behind. Players put their chips in the rails and then start betting for hours on end, always putting their winning chips back into the rails. With the fast-paced action on the crap table, it's difficult for the average player to discipline himself to skip one shooter and count his chips to find out how much he is ahead or behind. In blackjack, you have that opportunity when the dealer reshuffles. In roulette, it's a slow enough game that this is never a problem. But with craps, players should choose a method to limit their playing time in order to have a stopping point for determining the status of their bankrolls.

There are two ways to accomplish this. The first method, advocated by the late Sam Grafstein ("the Dice Doctor"), is to use a betting fund with lockup chips. I've found this method an excellent way to pace myself at the crap table. Line up your chips in the front rails. Your starting bankroll is the betting fund to make your bets. When you win a bet, pick up all your chips and then use these chips (kept in your hand) to make your next series of bets on the table. When you've accomplished this, take whatever chips are left in your hand and lock them up by putting them in the rails behind your betting fund.

If you use this method of money management, you limit your playing to the time it takes to wager all the chips in the betting fund. When this is accomplished, you stop playing to count up all the chips in your lockup rack. If the amount of money exceeds what you started with, then keep playing (move the chips back to the betting fund). If instead the amount locked up is less than what you started with, then maybe it's time to quit that table, move on, and try your luck at another.

An alternative to this method of money management was proposed by Bill Jones (*The New Easy Way to Win at Craps*). Here, you make all your bets from the betting fund and when you win, you first place all the chips you used to make the original bets back into the betting fund, then place what's left into the separate lockup fund.

Both of these techniques will discipline you to stop and evaluate the condition of your bankroll after a period of time. They also can be used to determine if it might not be better to quit a winner or quit for another table. Use these general guidelines.

When you've exhausted your betting fund, quit your session if: a. Your lockup fund is 50% more than the original betting fund (quit a winner) or b. Your lockup fund is less than the original betting fund (quit, take a break, and then try another table).

Use these concepts with the techniques of knowing how to bet, where to bet and how to increase your bets, and you'll soon find yourself losing a lot less and winning a lot more.

◆ ◆ ◆

The "Dumb" Crap Player

A typical "dumb" crap player - one that the casinos love to cater to - bets the following way. After getting a marker or IOU for a thousand or so dollars worth of casino chips, he places a pile of chips on the pass line. When a point is established he throws another bunch of chips on the table and instructs the dealer he wants all the numbers covered except the point number. He also proceeds to toss a couple chips to the stickperson to put on the point number as a hardway bet and maybe even a two way CE bet, or if he really feels lucky another few chips on the "yo". Naturally when his number hits he instructs the dealer to press his bets. And often when things aren't going his way, he'll increase his betting level as a way to quickly recoup his losses. This type of player looks impressive at the table as he barks out instructions to the dealer and tosses chips to the stickperson almost non-stop between dice throws. Dealers cater to these players because they often tip them very well.

Sometimes these players win big when a hot roll occurs. But more often than not, they end up big losers.

It's tempting to bet a few chips on the hardways or other proposition bets. But you are a fool or absolutely crazy to consistently do so with the astronomical casino edge these bets command.

To be a consistent winner at craps, you must lay off the bets with a high casino advantage and stick to making bets with the lowest possible casino advantage such as the pass/don't pass with odds, come/don't come with odds, and the 6 and 8 place bets. By doing so, you will be winning more money over time vs making bets with a high casino edge.

Smart players do the following:

1. They develop a game plan before heading for their favorite casino. This includes knowing which bets they will make at what betting level, with what bankroll, and when to quit.

2. They study up on the game of craps and know which are the best bets, the ones with the lowest casino edge.

3. The smart player never bets more when losing, rather he gradually increases his betting level on consecutive wins.

4. The smart player never limits the amount that can be won on any session - he never quits on a winning streak.

5. The smart player divides his bankroll into mini-session bankrolls and sets loss limits on each session. If he loses a session bankroll, he quits.

6. The smart player learns that when he is ahead and the tide turns that is the time to "take the money and run". He never loses his profits (a cardinal sin in gambling).

Don't be a dumb crap player; stick with the bets with the lowest casino edge, learn proper money management, and become a smart player.

◆ ◆ ◆

4

Slots

Slot Machine Misconceptions

By far the largest segment of casino players are those who play the slots. This wasn't always the case. Twenty-five years ago when I first visited Las Vegas, the vast majority of individuals who played the slots were the female companions of male table players. It was common to see the husband at the crap table peel off a few twenty dollar bills from his bankroll and hand it to his wife so she could amuse herself playing the slots while he did the serious playing. In fact back then no respectable table player would want to be caught playing the slots. But then a funny thing happened. Slot machine manufacturers saw the phenomena that was occurring with kid's video games (i.e. Nintendo) and began to produce a new line of slot machines that contained computer chips, vivid graphics, even sound effects. And to add excitement they offered big million dollar slot jackpots and boldly advertised "one pull could change your life".

Casino managers' approach to slot machine players gradually began to change when more and more of the bottom line revenue was being generated from them. Table players used to be the only players who received complimentary dinners, show tickets, rooms, even transportation depending upon how much they were willing to risk at the tables. Nowadays casino revenues from slot machines often exceed the revenues from the traditional games of blackjack, craps, roulette and baccarat. Casinos now go to great lengths to cater to and reward the slot machine players. Atlantic City casinos popularized the frequent slot player rewards programs that are now being used by most casinos in the USA. The concept was simple and mirrored the frequent flyer programs developed by the airlines; namely, simply reward those players who frequently play the slots. Computer technology made tracking the play of a slot machine player easy. It's relatively easy to obtain a slot machine player card from any casino (just ask any attendant and they will point you to an area where you can simply fill out a form and usually within a few minutes obtain your card). You then insert your card into the card reader located on every slot machine. This card identifies you as the player of this machine and the computer will track how much money you put into the machine. The more frequently you play the slots the more rewards the casino will return to you in the form of cash, free merchandise, free invitations to special events, etc.

With so many individuals playing the slots these days and trying to figure out how to beat them, it's not surprising that a whole myriad of misconceptions about them has evolved. Here are several of these misconceptions and my responses.

"Once a slot machine pays off a big jackpot, don't play it because it won't hit again for some time." The converse to this is "only play a slot machine that is due to hit." The problem with this theory is that neither you nor for that matter the slot machine knows when it's due to hit. You see, slot machines are now run by a computer chip that randomly selects the symbols that appear on the screen. These so-called random number generator computer chips can't keep track of what has happened

in the past and like their name implies, they do their thing in a completely random way.

Whether a slot machine has just paid off a big jackpot on the previous pull or it hasn't paid off in the last hundred pulls, has no bearing on the very next pull. The odds if you wish of hitting it big remain the same on each pull.

"Slot machines near entrances to casinos pay off more than other machines." I was told many years ago from several casino managers in Las Vegas that this was sometimes done to attract individuals to "come in and play". Nothing will entice someone to play the slots more than the clanking of winning coins dropping into the pan with blinking lights and bells. Nowadays, however, casinos don't need to lure individuals to play slots so the marketing ploy of putting higher paying slots near entrances is rarely used except on riverboats. What seems to be the trend is to put the looser slots (those that pay more) in an area of the casino that has high visibility (like carousels at the end of an aisle of machines).

"Casinos can change the payoffs on the slot machines. Be especially leery of the slot mechanic fiddling around the inside of the machine." The payoffs on every slot machine are coded if you wish on the computer chip that's inserted in the machine when it's manufactured. Casinos, slot technicians, etc. cannot alter the payoffs.

"Ask a slot attendant which machines are paying off better than others." While there is some truth to this, it has to do with the payback percentages the casinos decide to implement on their various denomination slot machines. As a general rule, higher denomination slot machines-such as $1.00 and up machines-pay back more than the lower denomination 50, 25, and 5 cent machines. Just because a specific dollar machine has paid off more frequently in the last hours vs an adjacent similar machine is no guarantee that it will continue to do so since you start pulling the handle or pushing the buttons (remember it's a completely random process).

"If a slot machine advertises a 98% payback then I

should expect a return of $98 for every $100 I put into the machine". These pay back percentages that you'll see casinos advertise are long term percentages. And long term is more than the time it took for you to put $100 into the machines. The expectations from a statistical standpoint is a return of 98% but in actuality a machine could pay back a lot less or even a lot more for each $100 played. It's like flipping a coin. After 100 flips you expect 50 heads but in reality you may have more or less than 50 heads. But the more times you carry out your 100 flip trials, the closer you'll get to the expected 50% heads (likewise the slot machines over time approach their expected 98% pay back).

Much to the chagrin of most slot machine players who don't like to hear this, there is really no way to consistently beat these machines. The best you can hope for is to get lucky and if you hit one or more large payoffs be smart enough to leave with your winnings. By all means use your slot card and take advantage of the rewards the casino will give you for playing. But keep in mind, the odds are stacked against you in a completely random game in which the casino has the edge.

♦ ♦ ♦

How Slot Machines Work

I was recently a guest on a radio show in the Mississippi Gulf Coast area and several questions had to do with how slot machines work and if casinos can "fix" a slot machine payoff.

In the old days when slot machines were mechanical, if you knew how many different symbols there were on each reel then it was easy to calculate the probability of winning. A typical reel had 20 symbols, the common cherry, oranges, bells, etc. If the slot machine had one jackpot symbol on each reel then the odds of those three jackpot symbols lining up on the payline was easy to calculate. In fact the probability was simply 1/20 times 1/20 times 1/20 or about 7999 to 1 odds. The introduction of the new, modern, computer controlled slots has changed all this.

Nowadays, slot machines contain tiny computer chips with a random number generator. The latter randomly generates a series of numbers every millisecond even when the slot machine is idle. These randomly generated numbers are correlated to the different symbols on the reel. However this correlation is not 1 to 1. The casino can have the slot machine manufacturer program this correlation between the random number and the probability of the symbol lining up on the payline. Thus unlike the mechanical machines where each symbol had an equal probability of showing on the payline, with the new slot machines the probability can be adjusted so that some symbols have a higher chance of showing than others.

This programming gives casinos a lot of flexibility on how to set it's advantage. Based on how it programs the probability of the winning symbols to show on the payline and the amount of payback, it can set machines to have a high casino edge or a relatively low one. In fact, a specific machine may, for example, be set to return 92% and by reprogramming the correlation or probability of those symbols showing on the payline, the same machine can be programmed to a higher or lower return rate.

From the player's perspective all that really matters is that the outcome of each handle pull is a completely random process (that is the purpose of the RNG). What this means is that it doesn't make one iota of difference what the previous results were on a specific machine, or how many coins are played, or who is pulling the slot handle. You cannot predict what is about to happen when you put your coins into the acceptor. Even if someone just hit the jackpot on a specific machine, the probability remains the same that the jackpot could hit on the next play.

The best you can do as a smart casino player is play on machines in gambling jurisdictions that historically pay back more and to budget your money wisely when you play the slots.

Several casino publications, such as *Casino Player Magazine*, summarize the slot paybacks for casinos in different parts of the country. In Las Vegas, for example, the slot machines in the downtown area historically have paid better then the machines in casinos along the strip.

My advice to slot players is to always join the casino's frequent players club so that part of your investment in the slot machines will be returned to you in cash rebates and comps. Also, you may want to consider entering a slot tournament where you have just as much chance as the next guy to walk away with the jackpot.

◆ ◆ ◆

Ten Tips for Smart Slot Play

Too many slot players take the "how long will it last approach" to playing the machines. You take your playing bankroll and play the slots until you run out of money. If you are lucky, your money will last until you have to leave. This is a defeatist attitude so it's no wonder these players lose.

Is there a scientific way to play the machines? I was once told "people who consistently win at slots by playing them scientifically are called casino owners." That's because slot machines are programmed to return a certain percentage of coins put into them over a long period of time. There are no playing systems that will allow you to beat the slots over the long term. But over the short term, a player who knows how to play the machines smartly, will have a much better chance of decreasing his risk and increasing his chances of walking away from the machine a winner.

Following are my ten tips for smart slot play. It is the best advice I can give a slot player who is serious about playing, winning, and getting the most value from his investment.

Tip #1. Pick Thy Machine

Casinos offer two different types of slot machines. Some have very large jackpots while others have smaller jackpots (e.g. 5,000 coins or less). Although most players dream of winning a million dollar Megabuck Jackpot, the fact of the matter is that these high jackpot machines also have a higher "drain", which means your expected losses are higher when you don't hit the top prize. The casino's payback percent between jackpots, therefore, is relatively low (ca. 90%) which is not a good bet over the short term.

Slot machines that have smaller jackpots usually have a higher hit frequency which makes them a better bet over the short term. Casino managers agree. According to Richard Sheer, V. P. Slot Operations at New York New York Casino, "players do not like dry spells without a payout so they prefer the lower jackpot but higher hit frequency machines".

So how do you get the most bang from your bucks when playing the slots? For starters, try to play on slot machines that certify at least a 98% or higher payback or return. According to Mr. Keith Williams, Director of Slots Operations at the Stratosphere Casino in Las Vegas, "we have taken a bold approach by offering guaranteed paybacks on every slot machine. All of our slot machines are at or over 98% payback. And that's not just a few machines, that's all the machines. Other casinos advertise "up to 98% payback, whereas all our dollar machines pay back 98%". The Grand Casino in the Mississippi market is another example of a casino offering certified 98% return slot machines. They are the highest returns you will find advertised on any slot machine.

But what if you are at a casino that doesn't advertise or certify their paybacks? My advice is to play the more popular slot machines. Why? Because one of the reasons these machines are so popular is that they most likely have higher paybacks than the industry average.

In a poll I took of 6 slot managers from Las Vegas, the Chicago area, and the South stated the most popular slot machines are Red, White and Blue; Double and Triple Diamonds and Five Times Pay.

Location also determines to some extent where to find the higher return machines. The downtown casinos in Las Vegas, for example, consistently offer a higher return for their quarter and dollar slots than other areas. The national gaming publication, *Casino Player Magazine*, lists the returns for different denomination slot machines for several gaming jurisdictions in the USA.

Tip #2 Play Max Coins

Most slot machines are programmed to pay off a certain amount for each coin played. When you insert two coins, the payoffs are doubled. Likewise with 3 coins the payoffs increase proportionately to 3 times the 1 coin pay out. However, the jackpot on most slot machines increases to bonus levels with maximum coins played. Always check if this is the case before you play the machine. How do you do this? Just glance at the payoffs listed somewhere on the machine. If the jackpot pays 1,000 coins for first coin played, 2,000 for 2 coins but 5,000 coins for 3 coins, then it's important that you play the maximum of 3 coins. If you play less than 3 coins in these machines the overall return percentage is significantly lower compared to maximum coins played.

Tip #3 More is Better

It's no secret that the higher the denomination machine the higher the return percentages. On average, quarter machines pay back 91-96%, whereas dollar and five dollar machines pay back more. Therefore to maximize your chances of leaving a winner, playing at a higher denomination machine is your best bet. Putting a single dollar in a dollar machine (ideally one that doesn't offer a bonus for a maximum coin jackpot) is a better bet than putting 3 quarters in a quarter machine. But you stand to lose more money at the higher limit machines unless you do what my fellow writer, Frank Scoblete, suggests, which is to slow down your play by pausing in between handle pulls. It takes discipline but if you can do it, you will be reducing your risk and increasing your chances of going home a winner.

Tip #4 Manage Your Money

First, divide the money you've set aside for playing the slots into 2 or 3 playing sessions. Do not risk blowing it all in one session! If your first session is a bummer, give it a rest before you start your next session.

To keep yourself in control when you play, I suggest trying a slot money management system I developed called the *Pocket The Profit Slot System.* If you use it when you play the slots, you will be amazed how many times you will go home a winner instead of a consistent loser.

Some slot players prefer to use coins whereas others prefer to spin using machine credits. I've described the system for both methods of play.

Using coins.
1. Buy a roll of coins with your first session bankroll and place the coins in a slot cup. This is your playing bankroll.

2. Play all the coins into a high return machine making sure you don't combine any winnings with your playing bankroll.

3. Count up how many coins you have in the slot pan. If you have less coins than when you started, you are obviously behind. Put the coins into a slot cup and repeat the process, only do so at a different high return slot machine.

4. If you have more coins then when you started with you are obviously ahead. Take your original bankroll plus 10% of your profits (1 out of 10 coins) and pocket it. Put the remaining coins into the slot cup and play them through the slot machine. At this point, you've got your original bankroll plus a little profit locked up and you are playing with your winnings.

5. After you've played your winnings through the machine, add up the coins in the slot pans and pocket half of them. The other half can be played through the machine again.

6. Continue to repeat step 5 until you run out of coins. But don't fret because if you've followed the system, you've got your starting bankroll plus profits socked away.

If you preload a slot machine with bills, then you need to count every time you hit the spin button. For example, suppose you preload a $1 machine with $90. The machine will register 90 credits. If you are playing 3 credits per spin then you have enough credits to spin the reels 30 times ($90 divided by 3). Simply spin the reels a total of 30 times which is equivalent to playing your starting bankroll once through the machine. Check the amount of credits you have after the 30 spins. If you have more than 90 credits, cash out and pocket the starting bankroll of $90 plus 10% of the profits and put the left over coins through the machine following steps 5 and 6 above.

Tip #5 Play The Carousels

If you are not playing certified slot machines then play those machines that are most likely to be higher paying. Where are these located? Most managers I've surveyed tend to place the higher paying machines "in highly visible areas" of the casinos. In large casinos these higher return slots are placed in carousels at the end of aisles. On riverboats it's at the entrances to the boarding docks. That's not to say you won't find high payoff machines elsewhere in a casino, but I'd play the machines in those areas first.

Tip #6 Join The Club

Casinos are willing to give you back a percentage of the amount of money you invest in a slot machine but only if you join a slot club. And not just any casino's slot club because they are not all alike. The better slot clubs offer a higher cash rebate than others. For example according to Bill Fishman, Director of Casino Operations at the Isle of Capri Casino in Biloxi, MS, "our slot club members who play $750 coin-in will receive 150 points worth $5.00 in cash rebate. That's a 0.67% cash return".

What does that mean? Suppose you play at a dollar machine with an expected 98% payback. If you add the 0.67% cash rebate return to the 98% return, your total return now increases to 98.7%. But there's more.

Tip #7 Play at One Casino

If you are a loyal member of a casino's slot club program you will be entitled to a lot more than just cash rebates. How about these perks: free meal comps, free or discounted hotel rooms, free invitations to special events, free gifts (especially on your birthday), free entry into casino slot tournaments, and invitations to special events hosted by casinos (free, of course).

And if that's not enough incentives, some casinos reward their preferred slot club players with special events that offer the chance for players to win thousands in additional prizes just for playing their favorite machine. According to Mr. Ken Lathrop, V. P. Casino Marketing at Treasure Island Casino in Las Vegas, "if you are an active slot club member and meet certain playing criteria, you will be invited to our "Give Away Weekends". "Players receive a ticket for a drawing that includes cash awards and luxury automobiles. Based upon your slot play or the number of hand held jackpots you get, you can earn more tickets. Some of our players accumulate 3 or 4 tickets for the drawing, while others have as many as 40".

Circus Circus Casino in Las Vegas has a similar program to reward their preferred slot players. According to Todd Simons, Slot Director, "we utilize our data base to invite our preferred slot players for jackpot contests on our 97.4% payback machines. They gamble with their own money over a period of time and the players with the most thousand dollar jackpots will get an additional 8 to 12 thousand dollar bonus on top of what they already won. Typically the customer who wins the bonus will have won 7 to 10 jackpots over a two-day period".

It's a good idea to shop around for the best deals in slot club benefits. One good source of information is Jeffrey Compton's "*Las Vegas Advisor Guide to Slot Clubs*". The book summarizes the benefits of Las Vegas casino slot clubs and which ones offer more.

It's not hard to figure that a slot player can easily earn 1% and more with the above cash rebates, perks, and other goodies. It's an excellent way of getting value for your investment in playing the machines.

Tip # 8 Know Who To Ask For Freebies

Get to know the slot hosts especially when you get hungry and want to eat or you feel like taking a break and seeing a show. According to Mr. Keith Williams, Director of Slots at the Stratosphere in Las Vegas, "we have a staff of slot hosts whose only job is to take care of our slot players. They are very liberal with buffet and show comps. If you are playing any machine you can get a show comp".

Here's a technique from Compton's book for asking for the comp. "Slot hosts are much more generous with comps than club booth personnel. After giving the casino about $2,000 in slot play, ask a change person or cashier to send over a slot host. Do not go to the slot club booth, but stay seated at the machine entrance. Hosts are much more generous when dealing with a player in action vs a 'beggar'".

Tip #9 Play in Tournaments

If you participate in slot tournaments you have a chance of winning big money - while enjoying free room, meals, gifts, and anything else the casino throws in as an inducement to play. In some cases, the value of all the freebies that you get for being a tournament participant will exceed your expected monetary loss. Just make sure that *all* of the players' entry fees are returned in the form of prizes. If you are not sure, ask the tournament director about this.

When you play in a slot tournament, you are competing against other fellow participants. The players who end up with the most machine credits after a specified playing time will end up with the prizes. Speed is important. You've got to practice tapping that spin button at a consistently fast pace. If you've never entered a tournament, I suggest you consider a one-day mini-tournament. The entry fee is lower ($50 or less) and the top prize is usually $500 to $1,000. Even if you lose, some casinos give away prizes equal to your entry fee. It's a good way to gain tournament experience with little monetary risk.

Tip #10 Common Sense, Willpower & Discipline

You've got to exhibit all three to play smartly. What does this mean? Don't play with any more money than you can afford to lose. Leave your ATM card at home. If you're behind, don't get upset or play longer to get even. The main reason most slot players lose is because they don't quit when they are ahead. Therefore, if the Gods of Chance smile on you and you hit the jackpot, for God's sake, scoop up those coins and walk away a winner!

◆ ◆ ◆

Hot New Slots

Having just returned from a trip to Las Vegas, I can report first-hand on several new slot machines that players are standing and waiting to play (yes, they were that popular). Some of these new generation slot machines have been or will soon be finding their way into other gambling jurisdictions.

These new slot machines are visually more appealing to players with enhanced graphics and sound. Some offer a game-within-a-game which makes playing them even more entertaining and exciting.

The Wheel-of-Gold or Double-or-Nothing slot machine was launched by Anchor Gaming and it continues to be a big hit with slot players. These machines contain a miniature big six wheel on top of them. Whenever a "spin the wheel" symbol shows on the third reel, the big six wheel is activated. The wheel contains bonus payoffs from 20 to 1,000 coins depending on where the wheel stops. In several casinos I observed crowds of spectators screaming and cheering for the lucky player who got to spin the wheel.

On the Wheel-of-Gold slot machines, players also have the option to "double their payout" by selecting the double or nothing option. Here the player bets that on a second spin of the wheel, the winning number will be either red or black. It's a 50/50 proposition and if the player guesses right, he receives double the payoff, if he guesses wrong, he loses his winning payout.

Adding the Big Six Wheel to the slot machine created the "game within a game" concept. Players can play the slots like they normally do but have the added excitement of extra payouts from the Big Six Wheel. The paybacks on these machines is about 90%.

IGT, the leading manufacturer of slot machines, recently introduced their Wheel-of-Fortune slot machines based on the popular TV show. These machines also contain a wheel mounted on top of a slot machine and also a sizable progressive jackpot (it was at a life changing $1,058,579 during my trip to Las Vegas and increasing).

Just about every casino that I visited on the strip and downtown had a bank of these machines fully occupied by players. These machines have unique sound effects including a simulated studio audience yelling "Wheel-of-Fortune" every time the wheel is about to spin.

Industry insiders claim that the payback on the Wheel-of-Fortune machines is around 88% including the spin the wheel bonus payoffs. Although the million dollar progressive jackpot is enticing, the odds of hitting the big one are about 50 million to 1. Although they are fun to play, the casino has a hefty edge over players.

The third popular slot machine on the strip and downtown casinos is the Odyssey slot machine by Silicone Gaming. This multi-game machine contains two reel slot games (Win-O-Matic and Dazzling Diamonds), a reel game with a bonus feature (Fort Knox), video poker (Phantom Belle), and two keno type games (Star-Spangled Keno and Krazy Keno). You've never seen graphics on a slot machine until you see the Odyssey's graphics. For example, a pair of ghostly white gloved dealer hands deal the cards in 3-D on Phantom Belle. You'll see full motion animation on Dazzling Diamonds. And if you hit the secret code in Fort Knox, well you have to see the animation for yourself to believe it.

Speaking of the Fort Knox game, here's a tip you can use. Just above the reels is a secret 10 digit number that represents the "combination" to the safe. Every time you put coins into the machine, you hope to match the first digit of the secret combination. After you match it, you hope to match the second digit, then the third and so on. When all 10 digits are matched, you get to pick one of three safe doors and win whatever bonus coins are inside that safe. Expert Charles Lund who is publisher of the *Las Vegas Freebie Chart*, claims that if you find an Odyssey machine where at least five of the numbers are matched, then you should play that machine at one coin per spin to complete the combination. If you follow this strategy, you will have a small edge over the casino.

I tried Lund's tip on a visit to the Grand Casino Biloxi last weekend. There were five Odyssey machines located on the second level next to the escalators. They were constantly being played but after someone left I checked the machine to see how many of the digits were already solved in the Fort Knox game (just touch the Fort Knox icon on the screen and the game will appear on the screen including the 10 digit combination). On the very first machine, I discovered 9 digits of the combination already solved. I played one coin per spin and after 14 spins, I matched the combination, picked the blue safe door and won a 110 coin bonus which I immediately cashed out. Later that same evening, I found another Odyssey machine with 7 digits of the combination already solved. It took a while longer but I matched the final 3 digits and won a 50 coin bonus.

◆ ◆ ◆

Slot Machine Jackpots

By now you've probably heard or read about the Birmingham, Alabama couple who had the good fortune of winning a five million dollar slot machine jackpot in a Mississippi Gulf Coast casino. The big win occurred on the morning of April 9, after the couple had invested about $50 playing the popular Double Diamond Megabucks Progressive Dollar Slot Machine. After playing the machine for about 10 minutes, when the reels stopped the couple knew they had hit something big, but were shocked when they finally realized just how much they had won. The next morning at a press conference the couple received their first check of $200,000 with 19 more installments to follow.

A slot machine jackpot this big is what all slot players dream of. Large jackpots of five million and more are only possible since the implementation of linked slot machines to a single large jackpot pool. These Megabuck slot machines can be found not only in Mississippi casinos but in casinos in Nevada, Atlantic City, Indian Reservations, and riverboats. A computer keeps track of all the coins that are played in all of these linked machines. A certain percentage of coins played are added to the increasing jackpot. The more players feed coins into these linked machines, the higher the jackpot as indicated by a video totalizer located above these machines.

Nowadays you will find linked progressive slot machines that can be played for nickels, quarters, half dollars, as well as dollars. As the marketing moguls of the casinos proclaim, "we have something for everyone".

Perhaps you are wondering how a casino can stand "losing" five million dollars to one player and still "survive". First, the monies are paid over a period of time so it isn't a one time hit. Secondly, the casinos are only giving back to one player a small percentage of money lost by many players who play those machines and help to "build" the jackpot. But more importantly the publicity of someone winning such a large jackpot more than makes up what the casino will be paying this couple. Remember the casino has a built-in advantage over all slot players. In the case of the Megabuck Slots, the casino will keep about 90-95% of all the coins that are played in these machines. The casino does not have to depend on luck to "win", they make their money based on the volume of play. The more players feed coins into these machines, the higher the volume of play, and the greater will be the casino's "win". And nothing does more to increase the volume of play than the publicity of a player winning five million bucks. These large jackpots are what keeps the players coming back. In the example of this recent five million dollar jackpot win, the casino has been jammed packed with slot machine players ever since. After all, if the couple won this money in this casino on these machines, I might get lucky like them.

Realistically, pouring money into a slot machine is a

losing proposition. So is playing a state lottery but this fact has not stopped the millions of players from buying those lottery tickets or feeding coins into these machines. One fact is clear, however. If you don't buy at least one lottery ticket or put a few coins into one of these progressive machines, you'll have no chance of winning these large jackpots.

I use the following strategy and logic when it comes to playing these progressive million dollar jackpot slot machines.

First, I set aside a very small proportion (about 10%) of the money I win playing blackjack every month into a fund that I invest in these slot machines. If I had a lousy month at the blackjack table, I don't play the machines. If I had a good month, I play.

Second, most slot players continually feed coins into a machine until they either hit a jackpot or lose it all (the latter is what usually happens). I take a different and more realistic approach. I use what I call a once-through-playing-system. I convert my bills into coins and play them once through the slot machine. I always use the casino's frequent player slot card and always play the maximum coins per spin of the reels. Once I've played all my coins, I immediately cash out. Sometimes, I end up with less than I started; other times I get lucky and end up with more. So far I have never lost it all. My worst experience was ending up with only 60% of what I started with. My best was doubling my initial bankroll.

This playing strategy at least gives me a shot at winning the big one, limits my playing time so the casino's edge won't eat me alive, and I get back part of my investment in cash rebates and "comps" given to me by the casino for using their frequent player slot card. Finally I don't end up losing my hard earned casino profits into these machines (remember I'm playing with part of my blackjack profits).

You are probably wondering how I'm doing with this strategy. No, I haven't won the big one yet. But over the past year I'm showing a very slight profit. Based on the casino's edge and the amount of money I've played into the machines, I should be losing. Fortunately, I've won several small jackpots which has kept me in the black.

Keep in mind that the only time I play these progressive machines is if I'm showing a monthly profit from playing blackjack. And even then I'm investing only a small amount of my profits into these machines in the hopes of winning the big one. It's a sensible strategy if you want to try your luck at winning the big one.

◆ ◆ ◆

Slot Club Basics

A reader sent me an e-mail wanting to know which casino along the Gulf Coast had "the best slot club". Unfortunately casinos can and usually do change the rules for their slot clubs depending upon marketing conditions, competitive pressures, and their overall business plan to attract and reward slot players. So rather than rate the current benefits of the different casino slot programs, I prefer instead to give guidelines that you can use to compare the benefits of your slot club vs others and some tips to maximize the benefits.

Some slot programs require an activation level before the casino starts giving out benefits. This usually requires a certain amount played through a machine before a player starts to receive benefits. Other slot programs require no activation levels. You start receiving benefits the first time you activate your slot card. Ideally a slot club program that doesn't require activation is a better deal so check with the slot club personnel about their policy.

Of course it's important that you ALWAYS insert your slot card into the card reader located on the front, on the side, or on top of the machine. Make sure the card reader greets you with a "Hello, Mr. Smith" or other greeting. This signifies the reader has accepted your card and functioning properly. If you don't get the welcome message, remove the card and try another machine. It's important that you get credited for every coin you play into a slot machine to reap the maximum benefits of the slot club.

What if you forget to bring your card with you? No problem. Just go to the casino's slot club booth (or ask an employee where it's located) and they will issue you a new card. Sometimes it's good to have two cards. If you are with friends and they do not belong to the slot club, ask them if they wouldn't mind using your card. While they play, you will be getting points to your account.

Most slot programs give players points based upon how much money is put into the machine. The latter is known as coin-in. It's the total amount of money you bet or put into the slot machine. Coin-in is not your bankroll. A player with a $100 bankroll might end up with ca. $800 coin-in depending upon how many times the player recycles his winning payoffs through the machine.

Casinos also use different countdowns which is the amount of coins you must play to earn one point. The card reader will indicate the count down. Some machines have a 30 coin countdown while others require more or less. Usually, the lower denomination machines (like nickels) have a higher count down than quarter machines.

It's important that you not pull your card from the reader during a count down, otherwise you lose all that play. If your machine requires a 30 coin count down, you should continue to play until the reader indicates a count down of 0 (or indicates you earned a point). Then and only then should you pull your card from the reader.

The better slot clubs offer a rebate of at least 0.5 to 1.0% based on coin-in. As an example, according to Bill Fishman, Director of Casino Operations, Isle of Capri Casino, Biloxi, "a slot club member who plays $750 (coin-in) will receive 150 points worth $5.00 in cash rebate". The percent cash rebate in this case is $5 divided by the $750 coin-in or 0.67%.

The percent cash rebate is a bench mark you can use to

compare one casino's slot club benefits to another. If you don't know what the cash rebate is for your slot club, then ask. The higher the cash rebate, the greater is your overall return. For example, if you are playing a reel slot machine with a certified 98% return, you would add in the 0.67% cash rebate to give you an overall return of 98.67%. But besides the cash rebates most slot clubs offer other benefits to their members. Many include:

1. Food and room comps based on your level of play (ask about the playing requirements).
2. Invitations to slot tournaments. The entry fee is waived and slot club members have a chance to win big money.
3. Invitations to special events. Many casinos are downsizing their slot tournaments in favor of member only special events. At the Circus Circus property in Las Vegas, for example, slot club members are invited to weekend jackpot contests in which they have a chance to win thousands of dollars in bonus cash awards if they end up winning more slot jackpots than their fellow players.

There are other perks to being a member of a slot club. Most casinos give away a prize or discount coupons just for joining. You also get VIP treatment like getting into buffets or shows via a special entrance to avoid the sometimes long line, birthday and anniversary gifts, discounted tickets to top name entertainment and more. If you add up all the benefits including the cash rebate, a slot club member could easily receive 1.0 to 1.5% return. Depending on the type of slot machine and its return, you could easily be approaching almost a 100% overall return. In fact astute video poker players who have mastered the playing strategy and are playing on a full pay machine (or one certified to return over 99% with expert play) will actually achieve an overall return greater than 100%. The casino in essence will be paying you to play. Therefore, it behooves you to shop around for the better slot club benefits because as a member, you have nothing to lose and a lot to gain.

◆ ◆ ◆

5

Video Poker

Want to play video poker? Before you do, you better understand the basics.

Which Machine To Play - All video poker machines are not created equal. Although the probabilities of getting a specific poker hand on these machines does not change, what does is the payback. For example, the most popular video poker machines are the ones that pay back if a player gets at least a pair of jacks or higher hand. Before you play these machines, check the payback on the screen. The highest payback machines are those that pay 9 coins for a full house and 5 coins for a flush for a single coin played. The five coin royal flush jackpot should be 4,000 coins. These machines are known as 9/6 machines and they offer you the highest theoretical payback for perfect play (99.5%). The 8/6, 7/5, 6/5 payoff machines yield a lower payback for expert play. Given a choice, play only those machines with the highest payback.

How To Play - This is the easy part. You can either insert coins into the machines or nowadays most machines will accept bills. The newer machines will total your winnings as credit which you can receive in coins at any time by pressing the cash out button. After you've inserted the coins, press the deal button. Five cards appear on the screen. You can select which cards to keep (or hold) by pressing the hold button beneath the respective cards. Pushing the draw button will replace the cards not held with new cards. In video poker, you can discard as many cards as you like (all five if you want). Remember the name of the game is to end up with at least a pair of jacks (or higher) poker hand for a payoff.

Rank of Hands - The higher the rank of the hand the greater the payoff. Therefore, it is important you understand the rankings. In descending order the rankings are: royal flush, straight flush, 4 of a kind, full house, flush, straight, 3 of a kind, 2 pair, jacks or better.

Payouts - The payouts for each of the above hands are listed on the screen. The maximum number of coins you can play is normally 5 coins. It is a good idea to play the maximum number to be eligible for the bonus payout on the royal flush.

Playing Strategy - The following is a very simplified playing strategy for the popular jacks or better video poker machines to get you started. Just start at the top and go down the list until you find your hand. The number in parenthesis indicates how many cards to draw.

You can also use this playing strategy on the newer double bonus poker machines. With these machines, you get paid a bonus for 4-of-a-kind hands but receive only a one coin payout for 2 pairs. The overall payback for machines which pay 10 coins for full house and 7 coins for a flush is 100.2% with expert play.

Basic Playing Strategy
4 of a kind or higher (keep)
4 cards to a royal (1)
Full house or flush (keep)
3 of a kind (2)
4 card straight flush (1)
Straight (keep)
2 pair (1)
High pair (3)
3 cards to the royal (2)
4 card flush (1)
Low pair (3)
4 card straight (1)
3 card straight flush (2)
2 high cards (3)
1 high card (4)
Draw 5 new cards
Never keep a kicker in video poker

Slot Clubs - It's a good idea to join the casino's slot club before you play. It's free. You will receive a card which you insert into a card reader located on the machines. A computer will keep tabs on how much you bet. After you've gambled a certain amount of money, you will receive free benefits from the casinos (everything from show tickets, meals, rooms, and even a cash rebate).

Money Management - Don't invest all your bankroll in one session. Instead, divide up your playing bankroll into several equal playing session bankrolls. Do not lose more than your allowed session bankroll in any one playing session. Also get in the habit of quitting for the day should you get lucky and hit a straight or royal flush.

There are other types of video poker machines besides jacks or better. They include deuces wild, joker wild, and others. The playing strategy is different for each game. My advice is to stick with jacks or better and learn the playing strategy for it. After you become proficient in playing jacks or better, then and only then would I suggest you try another game.

(Note: Here are two additional playing tips. If you are dealt 3 unpaired high cards, hold the 2 suited cards and discard the other high card. If you are dealt 4 high cards, hold them all except if 3 are suited - in which case hold the 3 suited and discard the 4th high card.)

◆ ◆ ◆

Winning Tips for Video Poker Players

I am continually amazed at the growth of video poker in casinos throughout the country. During my recent visits to casinos in Las Vegas, Atlantic City, the Gulf Coast, and midwest, there was hardly an empty video poker machine to be found. America's love affair with this casino game continues to grow.

Unfortunately, most players do not have a clue as to the basic playing strategies for video poker. Making incorrect playing decisions will cost you dearly. In this article I'll review some of the more costly mistakes I observe players making on the popular jacks or better machines and how to eliminate them.

First, do not hold a kicker in video poker! What this means is holding on to a high value card, such as an ace along with a pair. This might be a smart play to bluff your buddies at the Friday night gig into thinking you have 3 of a kind, but you can't bluff a video poker machine!

Resist the temptation to draw to an inside straight! You have probably heard this rule a hundred times but it's worth repeating even for video poker players. This is a costly mistake, don't do it. In the case of open ended straights, such as 5, 6, 7, 8, then by all means take a shot at the straight.

Always keep any pair vs holding a high card. This may seem
trivial but a lot of players would discard a low pair such as a
pair of 2's and keep one or more high cards instead. Do not do
this.

Always keep a high pair vs a 4 card open straight, 4 card flush
or 3 card royal. This may not be so obvious a play but it is an
important one that you need to memorize.

Always keep the low pair over a four card open end straight. In
this case a low pair has more value than going for the straight
and should be kept.

A 3 card royal should be kept over a low pair, 4 card flush and 4
card open end straight. The bonus jackpot pay off for the royal
makes holding the 3 card royal a better play.

Don't be afraid to draw 5 new cards if you have garbage. By
garbage I mean a hand that doesn't contain at least a high card
(or any of the other hands listed on p. 158).

If you eliminate the above playing mistakes and stick to
playing the full pay jacks or better machines that pay 9 coins for
a full house and 6 coins for a flush (per coin played) vs
machines that pay 8/5 or 7/5, you will be significantly
improving your chances of winning.

◆ ◆ ◆

Video Poker Hysteria

Last week when I was playing blackjack, I heard a
commotion behind me in the video poker slot area. When I
went to investigate the ruckus, there was a hysterical lady who

was upset because another player played "her" machine (when she went to get change) and hit a big royal flush jackpot on "her" machine. Her contention was that she was playing that specific video poker machine for quite some time and if she had continued to play she would have won that royal flush jackpot. I didn't stick around for the mayhem that followed but was this player right? What do you think?

The fact of the matter is that video poker machines contain computer chips that randomly select the cards that are displayed on the screen. In fact, these chips are programmed by the manufacturer and carefully checked by gaming regulators to ensure that the cards will be selected in a completely random manner. The actual part of the computer program that resides in memory in the computer chip that does the card selection is called the random number generator (or RNG). The RNG is always running and it randomly selects a series of numbers between 0 and 4 billion. Each series of numbers it selects (like 26931) corresponds to a specific poker hand (the five cards you see on the screen). It also randomly selects five additional cards that reside in a stack waiting to replace the cards that you discard.

The RNG "does its thing" every millisecond (that's one/one thousand of a second). When you put your money into the slot machine and either pull the handle or push the button, this action accesses the RNG. Whatever sequence of numbers (corresponding to a poker hand) happens to be in the RNG at that millisecond is the hand that comes up on the screen.

Now that you know this, it should be clear that this hysterical player I spoke about probably would not have hit the royal flush jackpot if she continued playing since it's the RNG that determines the timing, if you wish, of the jackpot.

You're probably wondering if it is possible to track the different hands that appear on the screen to determine a pattern that will allow you to predict when the RNG will select a royal flush. Forget it. This won't work because the RNG selects the "hands" in a completely random fashion so the pattern of hands that appear in succession will always be different. And even if you knew when the RNG will be selecting the royal flush, you wouldn't be able to play the machine fast enough to "freeze" that royal flush!

The only smart way to play video poker machines is to play those machines that offer the highest payback and then use a mathematically derived playing strategy that will have you make the correct playing decision every time (this is known as expert play). On jacks or better video poker machines, look at the payback chart on the screen for a full house and flush (one coin play). The greater the return, the higher the payback for expert play.

Machine Return	Machine Payback
9 full house/6 flush	99.5%
8 full house/5 flush	97.4%
7 full house/5 flush	96.3%
6 full house/5 flush	95.2%

The following chart shows payoffs for the newer 10/7 Double Bonus Poker machines.

Double Bonus Poker Payouts	
(Single coin)	
Royal Flush	800 (4,000 for 5 coins)
Straight Flush	50
4 Aces	160
4 (2, 3, 4's)	80
4 (5 through K's)	50
Full House	10
Flush	7
Straight	5
3 of a kind	3
Two pair	1
Jacks or Better	1

The 10/7 Double Bonus Poker machines are an even better deal for expert players. These machines pay a bonus for 4 of a kind at the expense of only paying even money (1 to 1) for two pairs. But even taking this into consideration, these machines return 100.2% for expert play when the full house to flush payoffs are 10/7.

◆ ◆ ◆

Playing Tips for Jacks or Better

Video poker slot machines can be found in every casino throughout the country. Even the new mega resorts in Las Vegas, dedicate a considerable amount of their casino floor space to these machines. And compared to regular slots, video poker gives the player the best chance at winning but only if the player has the knowledge of which cards to keep and which to discard. This week I'll review some of the more common video poker hands that seem to confuse most players and give the correct strategy which is the strategy that gives the highest expected return over the long term.

Let's assume you are playing the common jacks or better video poker machines and the following cards appear on the screen (the symbols d, h, s, c represent the four suits)

2d, 3d, 4s, 5h, 3c

If you study this five card hand, you'll realize you have two logical choices to make. Would you keep the pair of 3's or discard one of the 3's and go for the straight?

The correct strategy is to keep the small pair and draw 3 cards. You'll gain more in the long run doing this than trying to go for the straight.

This is a general rule that you need to learn if you play video poker. If your hand contains a small pair and also 4 cards to a straight, you should keep the small pair. The only one exception to this rule is if your 4 card straight contains three high cards (J, Q, K or Ace). If it does, your better play is to go for the straight.

Take a look at this common hand. How would you play it?

2h, 3h, 2s, 10h, Jh

Here you have two reasonable ways to play this hand. You can either hold the four hearts and go for the flush or keep the pair of 2's.

The correct play is to keep the four card flush and draw one card. Notice the difference in the strategy of the above two examples. In both cases, you have a small pair but in one hand you also have four to a straight and in the other case, four to a flush. As a general rule, you keep the small pair over going for the straight, but you'd keep the flush vs the small pair.

Suppose your hand contains four cards to a flush but also a high pair such as:

Js, Jc, 3c, 5c, 8c

Would you keep the jacks or go for the flush?

In this case, unlike the small pair example, you should keep the high pair. You'll gain more over the long term by keeping the high pair rather than going for the flush.

Players always seem to be confused as to whether or not to go for the royal flush. After all the royal flush yields the highest payoff.

As a general rule, if you have four cards to the royal flush, you should always go for it.

If you have only 3 cards to the royal flush, you should go for it only under these conditions.

1. You don't have a high pair
2. You don't have two pairs
3. You don't have 3 of a kind
4. You don't have a flush or a straight

If you have one of the above card combinations, then forget the royal flush.

For example, in the hand on the following page, you

should discard the pair of 3's and go for the royal flush.

10h, Jh, Qh, 3s, 3c

However if you were dealt instead:

10h, Jh, Qh, Jd, 3c

You should keep the high pair (J's).

Likewise the following hand contains 3 cards to the royal but also two pairs. Your best strategy is to keep the two pairs.

10h, Jh, Qh, 10c, Js

The above playing strategy can be summarized in the following rules. It is valid for the common jacks or better video poker machines and can even be used on the newer double bonus machines.

1. If your hand contains a small pair and four cards to the straight keep the small pair-except if you have three high cards.
2. If your hand contains a small pair and four cards to the flush, go for the flush.
3. If your hand contains a high pair and four cards to the flush keep the high pair.
4. Draw one card if you have four cards to the royal flush.
5. Draw two cards to a royal flush except if your hand contains a high pair, two pairs, 3 of a kind, straight or flush.

Study the above rules, follow them the next time you play video poker and you'll be making the correct plays.

◆ ◆ ◆

Playing Tips for Deuces Wild

Deuces wild poker machines get a lot of play because it is possible to get over a 100% return for expert play with machines that offer either of the following pay tables:

Royal Flush	800 coins	800 coins
Four deuces	200	400
Wild royal	25	20
5 of a kind	15	10
Straight flush	9	10
4 of a kind	5	4
Full house	3	4
Flush	2	3
Straight	2	2
3 of a kind	1	1

As a general rule, deuces wild is more volatile than the jacks or better version. This means you'll have playing sessions when you either hit a big payoff or come up empty handed. You can expect to lose over many playing sessions but when you win you'll win big. And if you are not a skilled video poker player you'll lose more over the long run playing deuces wild vs jacks or better.

You'll also receive a greater number of worthless hands (about 20%) in which you'll be drawing five new cards vs the jacks or better version (about 3% worthless hands). So don't be surprised if you must discard all your cards for a new hand in this game.

Since the four deuces are wild, they are the most important cards. In fact hands containing four deuces pay very well and occur fairly frequently (about once every 4800 hands) compared to the royal flush (once in every 47,000 hands).

Suppose you are playing a deuces wild machine and are dealt the following cards (the h, d, c, s represent the card suites)

7s, 7c, 8h, 10s, 8d

How would you play this hand? Most players would keep the two pairs and although this would be the right strategy for jacks or better machines, it is not the right strategy for deuces wild. The reason is because you need at least 3 of a kind in deuces wild to get a payoff. Therefore the correct strategy which gives you the highest gain over the long term is to keep one of the pair (either one, it doesn't matter) and draw three cards and hopefully end up with at least 3 of a kind or better.

How would you play this hand that contains 3 deuces?

2s, 2c, 2d, Jh, 7d

Unless you have 5 of a kind or a royal flush hand, you should always keep the three deuces and draw 2 cards.

What about these hands that contain two deuces?

2s, 2c, 5d, Jc, 9s

2s, 2c, Jh, Qh, 3s

In the first hand you should keep the two deuces and draw three cards. In the second case you are better off keeping the two deuces, jack and queen of hearts (four to a royal flush) and drawing one card.

As a general rule, if your hand contains two deuces you should draw three cards except if your hand contains a four card royal (above example) or 4 of a kind.

Here are some additional tips for playing deuces wild video poker.

1. Generally 3 card flushes, straights and high cards (unmatched) are worthless and should be discarded.
2. In general if you are dealt a pair, keep them and draw 3 cards. The only exception is you have 3 cards to a straight or royal flush.
3. Don't be afraid to go for the royal flush. Go for it if you have 3 or 4 cards for the royal.

Remember that the playing strategies for deuces wild is different than jacks or better. Whichever version you like to play, make sure you play only those machines that have the highest payoffs using the correct playing strategy. To learn more about expert play for both versions, I highly recommend the video poker books by Lenny Frome, Bob Dancer and Dan Paymar.

◆ ◆ ◆

$\mathcal{V}$*ideo* $\mathcal{P}$*oker 101*

I received this question from a reader on video poker slot machines.

"I read the books and see the casinos advertising video poker slot machines with 99% payback. This means these machines should return on average $99 for every $100 put into them. Well I've been playing these machines for over a year and I'm not close to a 99% return on my investment. What gives?"

First, when you read the books or see the casinos advertise 99% paybacks, this is feasible but only if the player plays at an expert level. The latter means for every hand dealt to you, you always make the correct playing decision that mathematically gives you the greatest long term gain.

The plain fact of the matter is that most casino players do not have a clue as to how best to play each dealt hand. By making "incorrect" plays, the player will be lowering his theoretical return from the expert player's 99% return potential to something much lower. That's why some casinos now offer and certify 100% payback video poker machines knowing full well that most players play way below expert level.

To give you an example, suppose you were dealt the following hand in a jacks or better video poker machine.

4 hearts, 5 hearts, 6 hearts, 6 spades, 7 diamonds
You have three logical ways to play this hand.
1. Hold the pair of 6's and draw 3 cards.
2. Hold the 4, 5, 6 of hearts (3 card straight flush) and draw 2 cards.
3. Hold the 4, 5, 6, 7 (4 card straight) and draw 1 card.
Which way would you play this hand?

The mathematically best play is to hold the pair of 6's and draw 3 cards. The second best play is to hold the 4, 5, 6, 7 and draw 1 card. The least desirable play is to try to go for the straight flush.

Even if you always make the correct play and played at an expert level, you will still most likely have more losing sessions than winning sessions. How, you may ask, can this be?

The answer lies in the frequency of hitting the royal or straight flush. The fact of the matter is that the 99% theoretical payback for expert play assumes you'll hit the royal or straight flush for those fat payouts. Unfortunately you can expect to get a royal flush about once in every 40,000 hands and the straight flush, about once every 9,200 hands. Therefore if you play a video poker machine even at expert level for a couple of hours, weeks, or even months and never hit a big hand you'll be getting a return that's less than 99%. If the opposite occurs, namely, you hit a big payoff after playing a short while, your payback in this case will be greater than 99%.

The bottom line is that most of the time even with expert play you'll be steadily losing unless you hit one (or more) big payoffs and recover your losses from previous sessions.

The best way to give yourself the greatest opportunity to win at video poker is to do the following.

1. Seek out the jacks or better machines that pay 9 coins for full house and 6 coins for flush (for each coin played). The five coin royal flush jackpot should be 4000 coins. These 9/6 payoff machines give you the highest theoretical payback for expert play (99.5%). The 8/6, 7/5, 6/5 payoff machines will yield a lower payback for expert play.

2. The new Bonus Poker and Double Bonus Poker machines have returns for expert play of 99.2% and 100.2% respectively. The machines pay a bonus for 4-of-a-kind hands.

3. If you want to play the progressive video poker machines that usually pay 8 coins for full house and 6 for flush, wait till the royal flush jackpot reaches at least $2200 (for quarter machines) or $8000 (for dollar machines). At that level of payout the machine's theoretical payback is about 100%.

4. Learn how to make the correct playing decisions to attain as close as possible to expert level play. There are plenty of good

books, computer software, and even an instructional video that will help you learn the correct playing strategies.

If you do the above and use a casino slot card to get credit for your play, you'll be getting the most return for playing the video poker machines. Unlike the regular slot machines which are pure luck, with video poker machines you can control how much of an edge you are willing to let the casinos have by how smart you play and which machines you play. Video poker is your best bet amongst all the different types of slot machines.

◆ ◆ ◆

Five Deck Frenzy

There have been several variations of the standard jacks or better video poker games that have been implemented in casinos over the past several years. Jokers Wild, Deuces Wild, Double Bonus, and others have hit the casino floor in an attempt to continue the love affair that players seem to have with video poker. But now comes the most radical version yet – Five Deck Frenzy.

Developed by Shuffle Master, the folks that brought us Let It Ride and the automatic card shuffling machines used by most casinos, this video poker game has several new twists including the use of five decks of cards instead of one and a life-changing progressive jackpot that starts at $200,000 and can quickly exceed several millions of dollars.

How did they manage such a large progressive jackpot? They joined forces with the leading slot manufacturer International Game Technology, who developed the technology for linked progressive slot machines (such as Megabucks and Quartermania). Using this technology they have linked all the Five Deck Frenzy games into one large network which allows them to offer the large progressive jackpot.

So what's the deal with five decks? Normally video poker slot machines are programmed with a single deck of cards. When you push the deal button, the game's computer randomly deals one card from the single deck to each of the five positions on the screen. When you discard one or more cards the draw cards are taken from the top of the remaining 47 cards. Thus, if you discard a 5 of spades from your original five card hand, you will not see another 5 of spades draw card on that hand.

Five Card Frenzy uses five independent decks of cards, each deck assigned to one of the five cards that you see on the screen. Since the cards are randomly drawn from each deck independent of the other decks, this makes for some very interesting hands that contain the same cards. For example, you could conceivably wind up with a hand that contains two or more of the same cards (like four 7 of spades). In fact, the progressive jackpot is all yours if you hit a hand containing five ace of spades (by the way, you could expect to hit the five ace of spades hand about once in every 15 million hands).

The possibility of getting hands with the same suited cards also creates additional bonus pay schedules besides the normal pay schedules. For example, a suited three-of-a-kind (like three queen of spades) pays more than a non-suited three-of-a-kind hand.

From the player's perspective the game plays just like the regular video poker game. The machine will take from one to five coins and you must play the full five coins to be eligible for the progressive and other high end hands. Because the progressive jackpot is such a large amount, I would not recommend playing this game with less than five coins (can you imagine how you would feel if you played one coin, hit five ace of spades and blew your chance at almost a quarter of a million dollars or more ??).

What about the playing strategy? For starters, you should use the jacks or better playing strategy. If you don't know it, then learn it. But there are some strategy changes because of the different format of this game. For one, you shouldn't hold a single high card (except the ace of spades) because the lowest paying hand is two pair. Secondly, don't hold two high cards unless they are suited. Third, always hold suited and non-suited pairs unless you have a shot at an even higher hand (as a general rule given a choice use this order to determine which cards to hold: suited pair is stronger than 4 card flush which is stronger than unsuited pair). For a complete playing strategy, I recommend Lenny Frome's book, *Expert Strategy For Five Deck Frenzy.*

What is the overall payback percentage for this new game? The experts claim a 98.3% return with perfect play and the progressive jackpot set at the minimum $200,000. That's slightly below the 99.6% to 100.2% return available on the better paying jacks or better machines. But as the progressive jackpot increases, so does the return percentage. Calculations indicate that when the jackpot reaches about $520,000, the machine's return will exceed 100% with perfect play. Also using your slot card when you play will raise your return percentages even more due to cash rebates and comps.

Will this new video poker game survive? Most pros don't like it because of its lower return percentage. According to the casino managers I've talked to, the play on these new machines is strong indicating most players like them. Personally, I'll wait until the jackpot gets high enough (about $450,000) to give me at least a 99.6% or better return before I give Five Deck Frenzy a spin.

◆ ◆ ◆

6

Roulette

Can You Beat the Wheel?

You can either play roulette on a bias wheel or an unbiased wheel. One of them is beatable, the other isn't.

Most casino roulette wheels are unbiased. This means the roulette ball has just as much chance to land in one of the 38 numbered pockets as it has another. Statistically, every number on the wheel should win on average about once in every 38 spins. Casinos pay winning roulette wagers at less than true odds so as long as their roulette wheels are unbiased, their roulette tables will generate a profit for them day in and day out.

In order for a wheel to be unbiased it must be manufactured to the tightest of tolerances and be perfectly aligned and balanced when used. Casinos go to great lengths to check their wheels periodically for any mechanical imperfections. They do this because as long as the wheel is perfect and the game random, they will always have the edge over roulette players. In other words, an unbiased wheel is virtually unbeatable.

But what about a biased wheel? Do they exist and can you beat roulette playing on it? Read this true story to find out.

It was in the late spring of 1986 when a friend of mine working in Atlantic City called and said a high roller was playing roulette with a bankroll of several million dollars. This intrigued me since normally high rollers tend to play baccarat or craps. Since I happened to be in the area I drove to Atlantic City to check it out. What I found might surprise you.

Two roulette players were placing $2,000 on each of five numbers on one of the Golden Nugget's roulette wheels. That's $10,000 a spin! I discovered the players had put up a cool 2 million dollars at the cage and had made a deal with the Nugget. They would play continuously until they either doubled their 2 million dollar bankroll or lost it all. The odds of the team winning 2 million was pretty small (about 3%). But guess what happened. After about a day and a half of continuously playing and betting $10,000 a spin the team had already exceeded its goal and was ahead not just 2 million but an incredible 3.8 million dollars. The odds of this happening are infinitesimal. But win 3.8 million they did. And to add insult to injury the same team came back to Atlantic City several years later and won another half million dollars at the Claridge and TropWorld roulette tables. All totaled the team won 4.3 million dollars playing roulette in Atlantic City (the team was headed by Billy Walters and his big win eventually made local headlines).

If you are thinking "they must have cheated" you are dead wrong. It turns out these roulette players learned what other astute players had known for a long time. Find a biased wheel and it's possible to turn the odds in your favor.

If you do the math you'll find it doesn't take much bias to give the player a substantial edge in roulette. The table below shows that if a number hits once in every 35.5 spins (instead of the normal 38 spins), a player would enjoy a 1.4% edge over the casino. Find a wheel where a number hits once in 30 spins and you've got a commanding potential edge of 20% over the casino!

Frequency	Players Edge*
38	-5.3% (American 0,00)
37	-2.7% (European 0)
36	0
35	2.9%
34	5.9%
33	9.1%
32	12.5%
31	16.1%
30	20.0%

*assumes a 35 to 1 payoff on a winning number.

Most skilled blackjack card counters would be very happy to have a 1.0% edge over the casino even under the best playing conditions. As you can see from the table a player has the potential to enjoy a much greater edge on a bias wheel.

So how does a bias occur? Usually it is a mechanical defect in the wheel such as a loose fret or a badly worn pocket that causes the roulette ball to land in some pockets more than others. In some cases these imperfections can be seen by the naked eye. Most of the time they can't. Even though casinos go to great lengths to check the integrity of their wheels, biases do occur and they can be exploited.

So how does a roulette player spot a bias wheel? That's the 64,000 dollar question. In fact the only way to know whether a wheel is biased is to keep track of the winning numbers to determine if some numbers are winning with a frequency greater than expected. And even if you find this condition you have to be certain that your result is statistically significant and not due to the normal variation you would expect in a random game. This usually means "clocking a wheel" (recording the winning results) for at least 1000 or more spins and then analyzing the results to determine if a bias exists. The greater the number of spins, the more reliable will be your results. During the time you are clocking you also have to be darn sure the casinos don't switch the wheel on you. Even though *teams* of players have used this technique to win large sums of money in the past playing roulette (see Russell Barnhart's book *Beating The Wheel*), this technique is not very amenable to a lone roulette player.

Or is it? Why not record the winning numbers for less than 1000 spins. In fact why not record the results from every spin and then analyze the results after every 38 or so spins. I know that statistically you don't have enough trials to determine with confidence if a true bias exists but let's try to use a little math to find a <u>potential</u> bias. What's the downside of doing this? *Nothing* other than you will be facing the normal casino's edge. The upside? You might just hit paydirt and find a bias wheel. Remember it doesn't take much bias to reduce the casino's edge and even swing it in your favor.

Let's suppose you record the winning numbers for 76 consecutive spins of the wheel. You would expect that each number would show twice on average (76 divided by 38=2). Suppose number 7 on your scorecard had won 4 times during those 76 spins. Is this an indication that number 7 is a potential bias number and warrant betting on it?

One quick way to get a rough approximation if number 7 is a potential bias number is to plug the number of observations or spins into the following equation and then do the math (this equation will give you the variance of 3 standard deviations from the average frequency).

$$n/38 + 0.48 \text{ x square root of n. (double 0 wheel)}$$
N is simply the number of observations or spins of the wheel.

Simply take a hand calculator and plug in 76 for n in the above equation and after you do the arithmetic you will wind up with the answer 6. In order for your number to be a potentially bias number, it should have hit 6 or more times in the 76 spins. Since it only hit 4 times, you should discount it.

The chart below summarizes the number of times a

number needs to hit in the specified number of spins for that number to be potentially a bias number. You can use it as an approximation for single 0 and double 0 wheels. Keep in mind that in the ideal world you really should chart at least 1000 or more spins before you can say with certainty that a bias exists. But we are not a team betting thousands a spin. We are out to have a good time playing roulette and maybe, just maybe, using our mini-clocking technique we will luck out over the short term and find a potentially bias number that will improve our chances of winning.

Number of Spins	Number of Hits To Be Potentially Biased
38	4
76	6
100	8
250	14
500	24
800	35
1000	42

Use the above chart when you play roulette. If your tracking comes up with a roulette number that wins equal to or greater than the number in the second column for the corresponding number of spins, that would be a target number to bet on. For example a roulette number would have to win at least 6 times in 76 spins for it to be considered a potential bias number. For 100 spins, a number needs to win at least 8 times. Certainly you are in a more riskier situation betting on a potential bias number with less than 1000 spins worth of data under your belt. But why not bet on these potential bias numbers? Even if the number is not the result of a bias you will only be facing the statistical casino's edge of 5.26% (or 2.63% in a single wheel game), nothing more.

When you use this technique make sure you use the up-to-date information to determine which number is a potential bias number. Number 5 might show earlier on as a potential bias number but after more spins another number may come to the front as a potential bias number. Bet on it rather than number 5. The greater the number of spins the higher is the probability that your lead number is in fact due to a bias wheel. If no number hits with the required frequency or if your lead number dies like a wounded favorite in a horse race, just stop betting but keep recording the winning results. Sometimes but not often you may have 2 numbers that meet the criteria of a potential bias number. If that's the case pony up and bet on both numbers. Sometimes you may have to switch tables if nothing exciting happens but with patience, your lead number will come forth and when it does go for it!

Most casinos have installed electronic scoreboards that record the last 20 or so winning roulette numbers. You can quickly scan several roulette tables to determine which ones have numbers that hit a least 2 times. Target that table and record the last 20 winning numbers on your scorecard. You now are ahead of the game and ready to start you mini-clocking.

Keep in mind that casinos check their wheels regularly for physical imperfections. You may on some occasions have to chart several wheels before you discover one that indicates a potential bias number. If you want to learn more about clocking a wheel and analyzing the data for biases, I recommend the book and accompanying software program (that does the calculations) by Mark Billings and Brent Frederickson (*The Biased Wheel Handbook*).

Since your goal in wheel clocking is to reduce or overcome the casino's edge, here is something else you can do to help. Play roulette on single 0 wheels vs those that contain the 0 and 00. If you do you will reduce the casino's edge right off the bat by 50% (from 5.26% to 2.63%) since one of the house numbers has been eliminated. Where single 0 wheels was once a rarity, nowadays most of the new mega resorts have implemented them. Even established casinos in their quest to give players the "best odds in town" have implemented single 0 wheels with low minimum bet requirements. Finding a single 0 wheel is not as difficult a task as it once was.

The last trick you should use to cut your overall cost of playing roulette is to use a player's card. It costs nothing and as you play you will be rated and a percent of the total bets you make will be returned to you in the form of comps. The net worth of the comp can sometimes turn a losing session into a break-even one or the latter into an overall winning session. Just don't overbet for the sake of a comp!

Are there other ways to beat the wheel other than to find a biased one? Yes, and following this article is a summary of a few techniques that players have tried; however, none have been as successful as playing on a bias wheel.

The bottom line is that it is theoretically possible to beat the casinos at roulette but to improve your chances of success you must clock at least a thousand spins or more on the same wheel, mathematically analyze the results, then if a true bias exists, be properly capitalized to take advantage of it. The mini-clocking techniques presented in this article are a short term playing strategy that will add fun to your playing experience and you just might luck out and discover a true bias wheel. You have nothing to lose above the normal casino's edge and potentially much to gain.

♦ ♦ ♦

Some Facts of Roulette

Here are some interesting facts about roulette.

♦ Starting with the number 0 at the 12 o'clock position, the numbers around the wheel alternate red and black. The number 0, 00 is opposite 0.

♦ Directly opposite every odd number is the next highest even number.

♦ Pairs of odd numbers alternate with pairs of even numbers around the wheel.

- Roulette chips have no value other than at the roulette table where you purchased them. Therefore you should never walk away from a roulette table with roulette chips in your pocket.
- Casinos usually use three different size roulette balls that measure 1/2", 5/8", and 3/4". Sometimes they will allow a dealer to select which ball to use.
- If a table has a posted $5 minimum bet, you must wager at least that much on a bet on the outside of the layout (e.g. red/black, high/low, etc.) If you wager on an inside number, you are allowed to spread the $5 over several bets so that the total of the bets on the inside numbers equals at least $5.
- The dealer marks the winning number on the layout, collects all losing chips, then pays off the winning chips first to the player who won on the inside numbers then to winning bets on the outside of the layout. The payoff chips for the winning inside numbers are placed in front of the player. The payoff chips on the outside bets are placed on the layout next to the original bet. Do not pick up these chips or make bets on the next spin until the dealer completely finishes paying off all winning bets and removes the marker that was resting on the previous winning number.
- Here's a technique you can use to check on whether or not the dealer has paid you off properly on a winning bet. Just mentally divide the number of numbers you have covered with your bet into 36 and subtract 1 from your answer. The result is the payoff. If you bet on a two number combo and win, your payoff is 36 divided by 2 equals 18 minus 1 or 17 to 1 payoff. This technique works for every bet except the 5 number bet on 0, 00, 1, 2 and 3.
  If you can't reach a location of the layout where you want to place your chips, just place the chips on the layout and ask the dealer to position the chips for you. Atlantic City casinos have the unique surrender rule. Whenever a player bets on a 1 to 1 payoff bet (that's a bet on red/black, high/low or odd/even) and the roulette ball lands in the 0 or

00 pocket only half of the bet is lost. This cuts the casino's edge from the normal 5.26% to the more respectable 2.7%.

♦ At $5 a spin on a double 0 wheel your expected cost to play roulette on a unbiased wheel is about $13 per hour. Making bets on a single 0 wheel on the outside numbers (or on the Atlantic City wheel with surrender rule) will cut your cost to $7 per hour.

♦ If someone else has already bet on your favorite number don't fret. Simply place your chips on top of theirs (remember roulette chips are color coded so the dealer knows whose chips belong to whom).

♦ Be careful how you position your chips on the layout since how they lie will determine whether you are betting on a single number or two or more numbers.

♦ ♦ ♦

Attempts to Beat The Wheel

Some players have attempted to beat the wheel by finding roulette dealers, who from habit, spin the ball and rotor with more or less the same velocity. Sounds crazy but when you think about it, most roulette dealers get into a routine or pattern when they spin the wheel and rotor over and over day in and day out. By knowing the orientation of the rotor at the moment the dealer spins the ball, it is possible to predict which portion of the rotor the ball will fall. The player then bets on the numbers that correspond to the pockets in this part of the rotor. There have been several reported cases of players cashing in on this dealer tracking technique (for example see Olaf Vancura's *Smart Casino Gambling*).

Another technique is based on the dynamic prediction of where the ball will land. Lots of differential equations are used to develop this playing technique. Basically if you know the time for one revolution of the ball and the exact position of the rotor when the dealer launches the ball, you can use differential equations to predict where the ball will most likely fall. Again bets are placed on an entire sector of numbers covering the predicted area the ball is expected to land. This technique is covered in the landmark book, *Beat Roulette With A New Patented Discovery* by Scot Lang (unfortunately the book is out of print) or in Edward Thorps, *The Mathematics of Gambling* (see also Olaf Vancura's book).

Still another technique using physics and sound (yes sound!) was developed be a German physicist and reported by Miron Stibinsky in his book, *Zen and The Art of Gambling*. The physicist was able to predict where the roulette ball would end up within a zone of 12 numbers by knowing the 1) the ball's relationship to the 0 on the wheel three rotations before it dropped and 2) the "clacking sound of a slowing spin".

Are there any betting systems to beat the wheel? Much to the consternation of roulette players the answer is no. There are no betting systems that turn the player's negative expectation into a positive one for an unbiased wheel.

◆ ◆ ◆

Don't Punt At Roulette

Being organized at the roulette table is very important. Many roulette players or "punters" as they are known in the trade, haphazardly make bets all over the layout. It seems they can't get enough chips on the layout before the dealer announces "no more bets". And if they are lucky enough to win a big bet, on the next spin they proceed to put twice as many chips all over the layout. Casinos love these punters!

It's true that there is no magic system to beat the wheel short of finding an imbalanced or biased wheel. Yet roulette is a relaxing, fun casino game which if played in an intelligent manner could lead at the minimum, to an extended playing time for your gambling money, or perhaps, a big win if you get lucky.

Here are suggested organized ways of playing roulette that will maximize your fun with minimum risk to your bankroll.

The betting methodolgy is called the Shotwell system. The strategy is to make only 5 bets on each spin so that you will cover the wheel within three spaces of every possible number. In other words, as you go around the roulette wheel the player will have a bet on every third or fourth number. Thus no matter where the roulette ball lands around the wheel, you'll have a bet in that general area.

The bets that you must make to cover the wheel in the above manner are as follows:

1 bet on the six number combination 1 through 6
1 bet straight up on number 20
1 bet straight up on number 26
1 bet straight up on number 8
1 bet straight up on number 10

By making the above 5 bets, the player will have the following numbers covered: 1, 2, 3, 4, 5, 6, 8, 10, 20, 26. These numbers lie three to four spaces from each other all around the wheel.

If the roulette ball lands in numbers 1, 2, 3, 4, 5 or 6, you will win 5 chips for the one bet on this six number combo. If instead the roulette ball lands on either numbers 8, 10, 20, 26, you would win 35 chips for the one winning bet.

In the event your six number combo bet (on 1 through 6) wins, on the next spin bet 2 chips on the six number combo (keep your straight up bets at one chip). If it wins again, bet 3 chips. Keep increasing your bet on the six number combo bet by one chip on successive wins. However, when this bet loses, return to the 1 chip betting level (increase your bets when winning, never when losing).

If any of your straight up bets win (pays 35 to 1) then on the next spin bet 2 chips on the six number combo (1 through 6) and 2 chips on each of your straight up bets. If any of your straight up bets wins again, increase all your bets to 3 chips. Again keep increasing your bets by one chip if you win but when you lose, revert to 1 chip.

If lady luck shines on you and you manage to win about 25 to 50% of your starting buy-in, then plan to walk with your winnings. Thus if you start with a $100 buy-in and you are ahead $25 to $50, consider yourself fortunate, pocket the profits and enjoy a dinner "on the house".

The above playing method for roulette is a sound, organized way to approach the game. It won't change the house percentage against you which is 5.26% on the American double zero wheel, but it will prevent you from becoming a "punter".

◆ ◆ ◆

Roulette Cancellation Systems

A reader asks: "*I was playing roulette and saw one of my fellow players adding and canceling numbers on a scorecard. He seemed to be winning a lot of money. Do you know what kind of playing system he was using?*"

The roulette system you observed is called the cancellation system. It has been used for a long time by European players where roulette is more popular. The playing system works like this.

The player writes down on his scorecard a series of any three numbers, for example, 1 2 3. The goal of the system is to win the sum of these three numbers, in our example 6 betting units, then start the system over again.

To play the system, you make your first bet the sum of the first and third number in the series. In our example you would cross out the 1 and 3 so that your series now looks like this: 1̶ 2 3̶. Your next bet is what is left uncrossed in your series which is 2 betting units. If this bet wins this first series is completed since all the numbers would be crossed out and you would have won the goal of 6 betting units (4 plus 2 units).

Let's try another series but show what happens if we lose a few bets. Your scorecard would have the clean series 1 2 3. You bet the sum of the first and last numbers (4 betting units) only this time the bet is lost. When a loss like this occurs, you add the amount of the loss to the end of the series so your scorecard now looks like this: 1 2 3 4. Your next bet is again the sum of the first and last numbers in your series only this time it's 5 betting units (1 plus 4 betting units). If this bet wins, cross off the 1 and 4 on your scorecard so your series would now look like this 1̶ 2 3 4̶. The next bet is the sum of the two remaining numbers in your series or 5 units (2 plus 3 units). If this bet wins, the series is completed and you would have won the goal of another 6 units.

In the event your last bet (5 units) lost, you would add the amount lost to the end of your series on your scorecard and your series would look like this: 1 2 3 4 5. The next bet would be the sum of the two end number in your series, or 6 units (1 plus 5 units).

What attracts roulette players to this system is the fact that when you win you cross off two numbers in your series, and when you lose, you add one number. This translates to a system that could show a profit even when the number of losses exceeds the number of wins. However, it is possible with a cancellation system to have situations where you never close the series. If this happens and you keep adding numbers to the end of your series, your bet size will be escalating. This is what ruins most roulette players- systems in which the bet size keeps increasing following consecutive losses.

If you want to try a cancellation type betting system at roulette you must put a limit on how large you want your maximum bet to be. If in the worst case scenario you hit the maximum bet and lose, then you should quit the session even though it will result in a losing one.

I still prefer to use a betting system in roulette in which you increase your bets following a win. These betting systems will have you increasing your bets only after you have won a bet. They are a safer and more conservative way to bet in roulette than the classical cancellation type systems. In my opinion it's the smarter way to play roulette.

♦ ♦ ♦

Betting The Outside Numbers

I like to make roulette bets on the outside of the layout. These are bets that pay 1 to 1 when they win and include red/black, odd/even and high/low. I particularly like these bets in the Atlantic City casinos because of the surrender rule. The latter cuts the casino's edge in half and is the smart way to play roulette in Atlantic City.

But no matter where you play roulette, the one betting system which has been most successful for me over the years when I play the outside bets is a system known as Oscar's Grind.

Oscar's Grind first appeared in Alan Wilson's classic book, *The Casino's Gambler's Guide*. I've modified the original system slightly and applied it to the even money payoff bets in roulette.

Normally I do not encourage players to use any type of betting system that increases the bet size following a loss. However, Oscar's Grind is unique in that the bet size is kept at the same level following a loss. It is also a conservative betting system with a goal of winning only one unit (or bet) on each series of bets. It's also a fun and easy way to play roulette since it involves varying your bets based on the following three simple rules.

1. Increase your bet by 1 unit following a win.
2. Maintain the same bet size following a loss.
3. Never bet more than necessary to recover past losses during a series plus a 1 unit profit.

The key to Oscar's Grind is rule number 3, only bet enough to win 1 unit to end a series.

The following table shows a series of consecutive bets using Oscar's Grind, whether the decision won (W) or lost (L) and the net profit (+) or loss (-) for the series.

Bet	1	1	1	1	2	2	2	3	1
Decision	W	L	L	W	L	L	W	W	W
Net	+1	-1	-2	-1	-3	-5	-3	0	+1

The first bet in series number 1 is 1 unit. You win the bet (decision W). Your net is +1 unit. Since you are ahead 1 unit, which was the goal of Oscar's Grind, set aside the 1 unit profit and start another series.

This second series starts with a loss. At this point you are down 1 unit. Because you lost the 1 unit bet, your next bet should be the same (rule #2). This bet also loses and now this series shows a loss of 2 units. Since you lost again, keep the bet size the same (1 unit).

This time you win. This leaves you down 1 unit for the second series. Since you won the previous 1 unit bet, you should increase your bet to 2 units (rule #1).

Unfortunately, your 2 unit bet loses. Your next bet should also be 2 units (rule #2). This bet also loses leaving you down 5 units for series 2.

Your next bet should be 2 units (rule #2) and the bet wins. You are now down 3 units for the series. You should next bet 3 units (rule #1).

Luckily you win the 3 unit bet and that leaves you dead even for series number 2. Even though you won the previous bet, your next bet should only be 1 unit according to rule #3 (you only want to bet enough to end a series with a 1 unit profit). This bet wins and you are ahead 1 unit for series #2. Set aside the 1 unit profit and start series number 3 with 1 unit.

There is a risk when using this betting system. A long string of consecutive losses could get you too deep in the hole.

To prevent this I use the following stop loss.

1. Quit a playing session when you have won one half of your playing session bankroll or

2. Your losses are down by more than 10 units and your next bet could place you down 20 (or more) units should it lose.

Practice Oscar's Grind on paper and convince yourself you can win small amounts. It's a good conservative betting system for those outside roulette bets.

◆ ◆ ◆

Betting The Dozens

One of the bets available to roulette players is a bet on the dozens. You can wager on the first dozen that includes the roulette numbers 1 through 12, the second dozen includes 13 through 24, and the third dozen, 25 through 36. A win will pay 2 to 1 meaning if you wager $5, you'll win $10.

I learned the following betting scheme for wagering the dozens many years ago and it has led to many winning sessions. You won't win every time you use it but with a little luck and the discipline to quit when ahead, you will find it is a pleasurable and often profitable way to play roulette.

You must first decide which dozen you want to bet first. Let us assume you start your betting with one chip on the first dozen (numbers 1 through 12). Rule number one: any time you lose a bet you always make your next bet the basic one chip wager. To put this another way, never increase your bet size following a loss, and as you will soon see, we will be increasing bets only after a win.

Let's assume you win your first bet on the first dozen. The dealer will pay you 2 chips as winnings. Take one of your winning chips and place it on the second dozen (numbers 13 through 24). Take the second winning chip and set it aside. Leave the original chip on the first dozen. You now have one chip on the first dozen, a second chip on the second dozen, and the third chip set aside. In essence you used your profits to make the second series of bets which covers 24 roulette numbers and still have the initial chip you started the progression with.

Let's now assume lady luck shines on you and the winning roulette numbers on consecutive spins are in the first and second dozen of numbers. You will progress your bet size following these wins as follows.

When you win the dealer will remove the one losing bet from one of the dozen numbers and pay you 2 winning chips for the other. Take one of your chips and put it back on the dozen numbers that just lost and set the second chip aside. Win again and the dealer will remove one chip and pay you two. Again replace the losing dozen number with a chip and pull back the second chip. From the last two winning coups you have two chips set aside. Take these two chips and add one to the first dozen and the second to the second dozen. You now have two chips riding on the first dozen and two chips on the second dozen.

If you win again, you repeat the process. Keep two chips aside and replace the losing dozen bet with two chips. Win again and you increase your bets on the first and second dozen to three chips. After three more winning spins you increase your bets to four chips on the first dozen and four chips on the second dozen. The progression continues in the same manner: 4 consecutive wins, then increase to 5 chips; 5 consecutive wins, then increase to 6 chips, etc.

As you move up the progression you will be keeping part of your profits and using the rest to gradually increase your bet size. After 4 consecutive wins you will have a 2 chip profit. After 5 consecutive wins your profit is 3 units and after 6 wins, it's 6 units. At any time that you lose both of your dozen bets, you revert to the basic one chip bet on the first dozen and start the progression over.

If you analyze this betting method, you will see that it involves increasing your bets following consecutive wins using part of your profits, a predetermined method of betting (dozens), and decreasing your bet size following a loss so you will never be chasing your losses. It is a smart and patient way to play roulette.

◆ ◆ ◆

7

Poker Games

Let It Ride

Let It Ride is an exciting new casino game developed by Shuffle Master. It has enjoyed tremendous popularity in casinos throughout the country because of these unique playing features:

1. It is an easy game to play and it is based on the all American game of poker.
2. Players do not compete against each other or for that matter against the dealer.
3. It is the only casino game where a player can remove up to two-thirds of his initial bet if he doesn't think his hand will win.

The objective of the game is to end up with a five card poker hand of at least a pair of tens or higher. If you do, you will win and the payoff depends upon the ranking of the hand. The higher the rank, the greater the payoff, up to 1,000 to 1 for the royal flush.

HAND	PAYOFF
Pair of Tens or Higher	1 to 1
Two Pair	2 to 1
3 of a Kind	3 to 1
Straight	5 to 1
Flush	8 to 1
Full House	11 to 1
4 of a Kind	50 to 1
Straight Flush	200 to 1
Royal Flush	1,000 to 1

The game is played on a blackjack size table with room for up to seven players. At the start of each game, each player must make 3 bets in 3 different betting circles or spots marked "1", "2", and "$" (these spots are clearly marked in front of each player). The fact that you must wager at least 3 times the table minimum on each hand is in itself quite unique compared to other table games. For example, if the table minimum is $5, you start each hand with a $15 bet. You would place one red chip ($5) in the 1 spot, another red chip on the 2 spot and the third on the $ spot. Even though you've wagered $15, you will see that you have the opportunity to remove or take down up to two of the initial three bets (up to $10).

After each player has made his initial mandatory 3 bets, the casino dealer will deal in turn 3 cards face down to each player and himself. The dealer's top card is burned or discarded and his remaining 2 cards become the "community cards" used by all players to complete their 5 card poker hand. (initial 3 cards plus the 2 community cards). There are no draw cards in Let It Ride.

Each player examines his initial 3 cards and based on the strength of the hand or potential to end up with at least a pair of 10's or higher, the player must decide to let the bet in his #1 spot ride or to take it down.

If you want to let it ride, you would tuck your cards under the chips in the #1 betting spot (like standing in blackjack games where cards are dealt face down). If instead you want to take down the first bet because your initial 3 cards were not particularly good ones, you would scratch the cards on the table (like asking for a hit in blackjack). The dealer would push your chip(s) in the #1 betting spot toward you.

After players complete their decision on the first bet, the dealer will face one of the community cards. This becomes the fourth card for each player. Each player must decide based upon the strength of the four card hand whether to let the #2 bet ride or to take it down.

To recoup, you have two independent decisions to make in Let It Ride. After inspecting your initial three cards you must decide to let your #1 bet ride or to take it down. After seeing the fourth community card, you must make the same decision for the #2 bet. You can, for example, let the #1 bet ride and take down the #2 bet or vice versa. Or you can let both bets ride or take them down. You are not permitted on your second decision to change your #1 bet (if it was pulled down it stays down and if it was let ride, it stays let ride). You have no decision to make on the $ bet. This bet always rides.

After all the players have made their decisions on the #2 bet, the dealer will face the second community card and then inspect each player's five card hands (consisting of the three initial cards and the two community cards). If your five card poker hand doesn't contain at least a pair of 10's or higher, you lose the bet in the $ spot plus any bets you let ride in the #1 and #2 spots. In the event you hold a pair of 10's or higher, you win the amount listed in the payoff schedule depending upon the rank of the poker hand. The $ betting spot will receive the listed payoff and each bet you let ride. For example, if you bet $5 on each spot and let the #1 and #2 bets ride, and you end up with a 5-card straight, each of your $5 bets would be paid $40 (8 to 1 payoff). That's a total win of $120 for the initial $15 bet. If you get real lucky and were dealt a royal flush with all bets riding, you'd end up with $15,000 for your initial $15 investment!

It should be fairly obvious that you should always let your first and second bet ride if your initial three cards were a pair of 10's or higher. Likewise you should let the second bet ride when your 4-card hand has the potential for a big payoff such as a 4-card straight, flush or royal flush.

A complete "expert" playing strategy for the game was developed by Lenny Frome, the author of several books on video poker. This optimum strategy which is contained in his booklet, *Expert Strategy For Let It Ride*, covers when to take down or let ride the #1 and #2 bets based upon the 3 and 4-card player hand.

Frome calculates a casino edge of 2.8% for Let It Ride. One caveat: this calculation takes into consideration the player will be dealt the high payoff hands, like the royal flush. Unfortunately these hands do not occur that frequently (expect to be dealt a royal flush once in every 65,000 hands). So while you patiently wait to be dealt a high payoff hand, your loss rate will be higher than the 2.8%. Furthermore, you'll quickly discover that about 75% of the hands will be losing hands (you'll be dealt less than 10's or better for no payout). What this all means is that unless you are lucky enough to get a high payoff hand when you play, don't expect to end up a session with profits. However, if you do get lucky and win a few high payoff hands, be a smart player, push your chair back and take your profits and run.

(*Note: Over the past several years, there was an optional tournament side bet available to all players. If you made the tournament bet and were dealt a royal and sometimes straight flush, you would be eligible to enter a regional "Let It Ride" tournament with top prizes in the millions (varied by number of participants). Shuffle Master, however, has recently announced they are in the process of discontinuing the tournament format.*

Another excellent book on Let It Ride has been written by Stanley Ko ("Mastering The Game of Let It Ride").

◆ ◆ ◆

3 Card Poker

3 Card Poker is a relatively new casino game. It is played on a blackjack-type table with a 52 card deck. Unlike regular poker where players compete against each other, all players at 3 Card Poker compete either against the dealer, or against a posted payout schedule for specific hands. As the name implies, each player and the dealer are dealt 3 cards. Players can either wager that their hand will be higher in rank than the dealer's hand ("ante" and "play" wagers) or they can wager that their hand will be at least a pair or higher ("pair plus" wager).

There are 3 betting spots in front of each player. Closest to the player is the betting spot labeled "play". Above it is the betting spot labeled "ante" and above it the betting spot "pair plus". These are the only bets allowed in 3 Card Poker.

After all the players make their bets, the dealer will deal each player in turn one card face down until all the players and the dealer have 3 face down cards.

The easiest way to understand the rules of 3 Card Poker is to think of it as a game within a game. The simplest bet to make is a bet on the "pair plus". The player wins a payout if the player's 3 cards are at least a pair or higher. The higher the rank, the greater the payout as follows.

3 CARD HAND	PAIR PLUS PAYOUT
pair	1 to 1
flush	4 to 1
straight	6 to 1
3 of a kind	30 to 1
straight flush	40 to 1

It does not matter whether the player's hand wins or loses when it comes to the payouts of the "pair plus" wager. It is a completely independent bet and the payout is based only on the rank of the 3 card hand. If you end up with a pair or higher, you win the amount listed above. If you end with less than a pair, you lose the "pair plus" wager. It's that simple. The second bet available to the player is a bet on the "ante". Here, a player will be competing against the dealer's hand. After the player examines his cards, he must decide on one of two options. They are:

1.   Make the "play" wager to continue to compete against the dealer's hand by placing gaming chips equal in value to the player's "ante" wager in the "play" betting spot or

2.   Forfeit the "ante" wager (and also the optional "pair plus" wager if the player made this bet).

When a player forfeits, the dealer will place the player's cards in the discard tray and collect the player's bets. The player is no longer involved in that round of play.

After the players have decided to either stay in and compete against the dealer's hand by making the "play" wager or fold and forfeit their hand, the dealer will face his cards. In order for the dealer's hand to qualify and compete against the players' hands, the dealer's hand must contain a queen or better. In fact, you will see this statement clearly written on the layout.

"Dealer Plays with Queen High or Better"

What this means is that if the dealer has at least a queen or higher poker rank, the hand continues. If the dealer does not have at least a queen (or higher) the dealer folds, the hand is over and the player's "ante" wager will be automatically paid off at 1 to 1 and the "play" wager will be returned to the player.

If the dealer's hand qualifies with a queen or better, the dealer will in turn reveal each player's three card hand to determine if it is higher or lower in rank than the dealer's hand. If the player's 3 card hand is higher in rank than the dealer's 3 card hand, the player will be paid 1 to 1 on both the "ante" and "play" wager. If the dealer's hand is higher in rank than the player's hand, the "ante" and "play" wager are lost. In the unlikely event both hands have the same poker rank, then the hand that contains the highest ranking card (ace highest, two lowest) will be declared the winning hand.

Depending on the rank of the player's hand the player may also win a bonus payout for the "ante" wager. In other words, if you get a good hand, your "ante" bet will receive a bonus payout as follows.

3 CARD HAND	ANTE BONUS PAYOUT
straight	1 to 1
3 of a kind	4 to 1
straight flush	5 to 1

The above ante bonus payouts are awarded <u>regardless of the dealer's hand and regardless of whether the player or dealer hand was higher in rank.</u>

Let's try a sample hand. Suppose a player makes a $5 "ante" plus a $5 "pair plus" wager and after seeing his cards makes a $5 bet on the "play" wager. If the player were dealt the highest hand, the straight flush, and the dealer qualified with a queen, in this example the player would win a total of $235 as follows:

"Ante" wager wins $5 (for having a higher ranking 3 card hand than the dealer).

"Play" wager wins $5 (for having a higher ranking 3 card hand than the dealer).

"Ante" wager is paid a bonus of $25 for the straight flush.

"Pair Plus" wager is paid $200 for the straight flush.

Lenny Frome, who has authored books on video poker and other casino games, states "the game is learned very quickly, since the basic playing strategy for players is simple: don't put up a "play" wager unless you have a queen or better". Based on this playing strategy, Frome calculates the casino's edge on the "ante" wager at about 2.1%, which is slightly lower than the simpler "pair plus" wager.

If you are interested in learning more about 3 Card Poker, I can recommend Frome's software program "3 Card Poker". For more information about it, write to Compuflyers, 5025 S. Eastern Ave. (16), Las Vegas, NV 89119.

3 CARD POKER HAND RANKINGS

The following are the permissible poker hands in the game of 3 card poker in order of highest to lowest rank.
1. Straight Flush - Three cards of the same suit in consecutive ranking with ace, king, queen the highest straight flush and three, two, ace the lowest ranking straight flush.
2. 3-of-a-Kind - Three cards of the same rank regardless of suit with three aces the highest and three two's the lowest ranking 3-of-a-kind.
3. Straight - Three cards of consecutive rank regardless of suit with ace, king, queen the highest and three, two, ace the lowest ranking straight.
4. Flush - Three cards of the same suit regardless of rank.
5. Pair - Two cards of the same rank, regardless of suit with two aces the highest and two two's the lowest ranking pair.

◆ ◆ ◆

Caribbean Stud Poker

Over the last several years, casinos have seen a decline in play for the traditional table games of blackjack, craps, and roulette in favor of regular and video poker slot machines. Table games once generated the majority of a casino's revenue; nowadays it's the slot department that is king. In their efforts to revitalize table play, casinos have been experimenting with new games such as pai gow poker, red dog, sic bo and others. However, the one game that has caught on like wild fire over the past year in casinos throughout the USA is the new table game, Caribbean Stud Poker, with its potential $100,000 plus jackpots.

Actually Caribbean Stud poker is not new. It has been played on cruise ships and in the Caribbean casinos for many years. Only recently it has broken through the cultural resistance to new games that was standard in Las Vegas. The Mississippi Gulf Coast, Atlantic City, several mid-west riverboats and other casinos have joined the bandwagon and now offer this exciting casino game.

What makes the game so popular is that it is based on the all American game of Poker. It plays fast and easy like blackjack and features a very large progressive jackpot like a slot machine. Unlike the regular game of poker, in Caribbean Stud all the players play against the dealer (or house) thus eliminating some of the intimidation that many players have about playing poker against other players.

The game is played on a table similar to a blackjack table with up to seven player spots. One deck of 52 cards is used. Prior to the casino dealer dealing the cards, all players must make an ante wager (usually five dollars but can be more). Once all the ante wagers are make by players, the dealer will deal five cards face down to each player. The dealer also receives five cards, however, one card is face up for all the players to see and the other four cards are face down. Each player picks up his five cards and makes a decision whether he wants to call the dealer or fold.

After looking at the dealer's card, if a player believes he has very little chance to beat the dealer (end up with a higher five card poker hand than the dealer), then the player can fold by throwing the cards face down on the table. When a player folds, the player's ante bet is taken by the dealer (i.e. player loses).

If the player believes he has a chance to beat the dealer, then the payer must make a secondary bet wager. The latter must be twice the ante, thus a player who made a five dollar ante wager must make a ten dollar bet wager. After all players have decided whether to fold or call, the dealer exposes his cards on the layout. In order for the round of play to continue the dealer's hand must qualify by having a poker value of at least ace, king or higher. If the dealer does not have an ace, king (or higher) then the dealer folds, the game is over and the dealer will automatically pay all the player's original ante bet at 1 to 1. The player's secondary bet wager is considered "no action" and the wager is returned to the player. After paying off the ante wager, the dealer will collect the cards and reshuffle for a new hand.

In the event the dealer does have an ace, king or higher poker hand then the dealer "calls" all the players' hands. The players in turn will lay their cards on the layout and the dealer compares his hand with the player's hand to determine which hand has the higher poker value. If the dealer's hand is higher than the player's hand the dealer wins both the ante and bet wager from the player. If instead the player's hand has a higher poker value then the dealer's hand, the player wins the ante wager at 1 to 1 and the bet wager is paid a bonus depending upon the value of the hand. The payoff for a winning bet wager is as follows:

1 pair or ace, king high	1 to 1
2 pair	2 to 1
3 of a kind	3 to 1
Straight	4 to 1
Flush	5 to 1
Full house	7 to 1
4 of a kind	20 to 1
straight flush	50 to 1
royal flush	100 to 1

Please note that the only way a player can participate in the above bonus is if the dealer has an ace, king or higher hand and calls all player's hand. If you have one of the above poker hands and the dealer does not have at least an ace, king or higher hand, you only win the ante bet (you win nothing for your poker hand because the dealer's hand did not qualify).

The best playing strategy to improve your odds is to always make the bet wager if you have a pair or higher hand. You should fold if you don't have at least a pair.

The major appeal of Caribbean Stud poker is a side bet that players can make in the hopes of winning the $100,000 (or more) progressive jackpot.

Prior to the dealing of the cards, all players have the option to drop a one dollar casino coin into the progressive drop slot located on the layout in front of each player. Note that this bet is strictly a side bet in which you wager one dollar in the hopes you will be dealt a flush or higher poker hand. The progressive jackpot payoffs are:

royal flush	100% of jackpot
straight flush	50% of jackpot
4 of a kind	$500
full house	$100
flush	$50

The jackpot increases as more coins are played into the progressive drop slot. Typically the jackpot exceeds $100,000 and an electronic video display above each table will indicate the amount of the jackpot.

Another point to keep in mind is once you make the optional progressive jackpot bet, you will win the current jackpot amount appropriate to your hand whether or not your hand beats the dealer or the dealer's hand qualifies. If your hand qualifies for a progressive jackpot be sure to inform the dealer. You will be paid the appropriate bonus at the completion of the hand.

Normally the jackpot side bet is not a good bet unless the jackpot exceeds $150,000 which it has on many occasions. Several lucky players in Mississippi casinos recently won about $170,000 on the progressive jackpot.

The casino advantage or edge on this game is about 4%. This makes it a better bet than roulette and most crap bets but not as good as blackjack. Still it's very difficult to win $100,000 playing blackjack but with a little luck it's a possibility in Caribbean Stud poker.

One caveat: there have been several cases where players have not participated in the progressive jackpot and were dealt a royal flush (what an ugly thought!). If you don't "drop the dollar in the slot" you won't be eligible for part or all of the $100,000 plus jackpot even if you are dealt a flush or higher. Therefore, my advice is to wait until the jackpot gets close to and preferably exceeds $150,000 before playing Caribbean Stud poker and when you do play don't forget to "drop the dollar" before each hand.

◆ ◆ ◆

Playing Tips for Seven Card Stud

Poker is finally making its debut in the Atlantic City casinos. The objective of this article is to review the basic playing rules for each of the poker games allowed in Atlantic City and to present some tips to increase your chances of winning.

The objective in poker is to win the money in the pot by either having the best poker hand or by forcing all other players out of the game. Poker must be played in a separate area from the main casino on specially designed poker tables that can seat up to eleven players and dealer. The cards used at the poker tables must be plastic cards and must be visually distinguishable from the cards used to play other table games (blackjack, pai gow poker, baccarat, etc.). You'll also see the poker dealers changing the deck of poker cards to a new deck every four hours (it's a regulation).

Unlike the regular casino games where the players essentially are playing against the house (if players lose, the casino wins and vice versa), in poker, players play against each other. In other words, the casinos do not participate in the actual playing or outcome of the game. The casino provides the table, the chips, a dealer and a pleasant playing environment. So how do they earn a profit? By simply keeping a portion of all the wagers made by players prior to giving the pot to the winning player. This is known as the rake. The casino can determine the amount of the rake (or what they keep) by either taking a percentage of the pot (normal rake is 5% of the pot), or they can charge a flat fee based upon the amount in the pot, or if they want, charge an hourly fee. In any event, every poker table must have a sign that clearly indicates the amount of the rake. Smart poker players shop around and play only in games with low rakes.

In order to play poker, you must learn the rank of the hands since this determines which player wins the pot. In poker games in which the high hand wins, the royal flush is the highest hand and a hand without a pair is the lowest. The ranking of hands from highest to lowest is as follows:

Royal Flush	A, K, Q, J, 10 in one suit
Straight Flush	Five consecutive cards in one suit
4-of-a-Kind	Four cards of same rank
Full House	Three of a kind with a pair
Flush	Five cards of the same suit
Straight	Five consecutive cards but not of same suit
3-of-a-Kind	Three cards of same rank
2 Pair	Two separate pairs of identically ranked cards
One Pair	One pair of identically ranked cards
No Pair	A hand with five odd cards

Cards are also ranked in poker. For games in which the high hand wins, the card rankings from highest to lowest are A, K, Q, J, 10, 9, 8, 7, 6, 5, 4, 3, 2. Thus three kings for example is a higher hand than three queens; likewise a pair of jacks beats a pair of nines.

In some types of poker games (known as low poker), the lowest ranked poker hand wins. In these games, the poker hand rankings are the opposite of the above rankings except that straights and flushes do not exist for determining a winning hand at low poker. Also the rank of the cards used in low poker for the determination of winning hands in order of highest to lowest rank is Ace, 2, 3, 4, 5, 6, 7, 8, 9, 10, J, Q, K.

All card suits in poker are equal in rank. Thus two kings of hearts have the same rank as two kings of spades.

Okay, so much for the basics - now let's get on to learning how to play the different types of poker games. As it now stands, the Atlantic City casinos can offer only the following poker games.

Seven card stud	(high, high-low split, and high low split eight or better)
Hold 'Em	(high)
Omaha	(high, high-low split eight or better)
Five card stud	(high)
Five card stud	(high, low)

Let's start by learning how to play the traditional favorite seven card stud, high hand wins the pot.

You need a minimum of two players and a maximum of seven or eight players. An ante is used in this game. This means everyone must make a wager in the pot prior to the casino dealer dealing the cards. (A sign at the table indicates the amount of the ante).

After everyone antes, the casino dealer starts dealing the cards to the player on his left and continues dealing in a clockwise rotation around the table. The dealer will give every player two cards face down and one face up. The player with the lowest ranked up card gets to bet first. All other players in turn must either fold, call or raise the bet. A player who folds throws his cards in and is out of the game. A player who calls bets the same amount as the previous bet made. And one who raises, bets more than the previous bet. After the last player responds to the most recent bet the betting round is completed and the dealer proceeds to deal another upcard to each player. Another round of betting occurs in which the player with the highest ranked poker hand showing, bets first or checks. The latter means the player does not want to make a bet but is still in the game.

In the event that two players have the same high ranked hand, the player closest to the left of the dealer bets first (or checks).

Once that round of betting is complete, the dealer deals two additional rounds of cards face up and then one round of cards face down to each player who has not folded. After every card is dealt to the players, another round of betting occurs. Poker pros use the term Third Street, Fourth Street, Fifth, Sixth and finally Seventh Street to indicate the round of betting. Third Street occurs after all players receive their first upcard (or third card dealt to them). Fourth Street is when all players have received their fourth card, and so on. The last card, Seventh Street, is dealt face down. A final round of betting occurs followed by the showdown or revealing the hands. The player with the highest rank five card hand (from the seven cards dealt) is the winner of the pot.

In seven card stud poker high-low split the player with the highest ranking five card high hand and the player with the highest ranking five card low poker hand split the pot. In seven card stud, high-low eight or better, a winning low hand may not contain any pairs or a nine, ten, jack, queen or king. In other words, the highest rank card in a low hand with no pairs must be 8 or less to be eligible to win the low hand. For example, a low hand of 2, 3, 4, 6, 8 is eligible but 2, 3, 5, 6, 9 is not.

When playing seven card stud high, here are some tips to improve your chances of winning. You should fold on Third Street unless you have at least a pair and if the pair is low, you should also have an ace, king or queen odd card. If you don't improve your three card flush or straight by Fourth Street, fold. If another player has a higher pair than yours, fold unless you also have an odd card higher in rank than the high pair. When you have a good hand play aggressively and raise especially if you have everyone else beat on the table. Don't stay in and chase other players - only the highest hand wins, not second best.

♦ ♦ ♦

Playing Tips for Hold 'Em, Omaha and 5 Card Stud

This month I'll conclude this two-part series on poker by reviewing the rules of Hold 'Em, Omaha, Five Card Draw and Five Card Stud Poker.

In the popular Hold 'Em poker, high hand only wins the pot (no low hand winner in this game). Each player receives two cards face down, a round of betting occurs, then the dealer places three cards face up in the center of the table. These are community cards (or sometimes called the flop) which are used by all players. A round of betting occurs, then the dealer places a fourth community card in the center of the table. Another round of betting occurs and the fifth and last community card is placed face up on the table. A final round of betting occurs followed by the show of hands. The player who has the highest ranking five card high poker hand using his or her two cards and the five community cards is the winner of the pot.

Players who bet last in Hold 'Em have a decided advantage over the other players. Players rotate, therefore, as to who bets first. This is done as follows. A flat disk known as a button is used to indicate an imaginary dealer. At the commencement of play, the button is placed in front of the first player to the right of the dealer. The dealer will deal the cards starting with the first player to the immediate left of the button. This player also is required to initiate the betting round. The player who has the button always bets last (remember, this is the imaginary dealer). After each game is completed, the button rotates around the table in a clockwise manner after each round of play. Therefore, everyone has a chance to bet last.

Here are some tips to increase your chance of winning at Hold 'Em. You should stay in a game if your first two cards dealt to you are A-A, K-K, Q-Q, and A-K or A-Q suited. Other playable hands are any two cards higher than 10 such as K-J. Never stay in if you have a pair less than 7's. You generally want to see all lower cards in the flop than the rank of your pair. Bet aggressively if you have a strong hand to force players out before the flop. Your best position on the table is to bet last which justifies staying-in with marginal hands. Finally, observe the play of your opponents to determine who tends to stay in with weak hands and who stays with only strong hands.

In Omaha poker, every player receives four cards face down (a button is used similar to Hold 'Em) and there are five community cards. Betting occurs after the initial four cards are dealt to each player and after each community card is dealt. The players form their five card poker hand by using two of the four cards dealt to them and three of the five community cards. This five card hand constitutes the poker hand of the player at the showdown. In Omaha poker high, the player with the highest ranking five card high poker hand and the one with the highest ranking five card low poker hand split the pot equally. The latter low hand cannot contain any pairs or a nine, ten, jack, queen or king (hence the term "eight or better").

Five card draw poker is played as follows. Every player antes and then the dealer gives every player five cards face down (again a rotating button is used to determine who is dealt first and who bets last). An initial round of betting occurs and once this is completed, each player in turn can draw new cards. The player is allowed to keep his or her original hand or discard as many cards as he or she chooses. The first player to the left of the button then initiates the final round of betting. Remember, as discussed in Part I of this article, players can either call (bet same as last bet), raise (increase bet), fold (drop out) or check (pass the betting option to the next player). The winner is the player with the highest ranking five card high hand. (In the five card draw poker low, the player with the highest ranking five card low hand wins the pot).

Five card stud poker is played to determine a winning high hand only. Each player in turn receives one card face down and one face up. A round of betting occurs with the player with the lowest ranked up-card betting first. The dealer then deals three additional cards face up to each player with a round of betting occurring between each deal. The player with the highest ranked poker hand wins the pot.

Here are some tips to increase your chance of winning at draw poker. For high poker, you are very vulnerable if you are one of the first to bet (first three of eight players). As a guideline, in this case don't open with less than a pair of aces or kings. If you are in position 4, 5, 6 (middle), don't open unless you have a pair of queens, and if you are in the best position (7, 8), only open with at least a pair. With low ball poker any hand with five odd cards beats a hand with a pair. Never stay in if you have to draw two cards. You should stand with your initial five cards if your high card is at least an 8 (if betting early) or 9, 10 (if betting late).

One of the keys to being a successful winning poker player is to learn when to fold. Players who stay in a game too long generally will be steady losers. I've said it once and I'll say it again: only the winner takes the pot-there are no prizes for being second best. Therefore, learn not to play cards that cannot win a hand.

And finally, it's important that you learn how to read your opponents. This takes skill and practice but after awhile you should begin to pick up clues that players make as to the type of hand they hold. Learning the patterns of fellow players is what usually separates the good poker players from the great ones.

◆ ◆ ◆

8

Imported Casino Games

Imported Action - Pai Gow Poker, Baccarat and Sic Bo

Once upon a time, a gambler didn't have many choices when it came to playing table games in a casino. You had your choice of blackjack, craps, roulette, and if you could afford it, baccarat. But times have changed and in an effort to stem the decline of table game play in favor of the slot machines, casinos have introduced a slew of new games over the past several years. Some didn't catch the interest or expected play of gamblers and have since disappeared. But three games popular in foreign casinos continue to be played with passion in Atlantic City. These games are pai gow poker, baccarat, and sic bo. The first two are card games, the last a dice game. Here's a breakdown of these games and how to play them.

PAI GOW POKER

Pai gow poker is a cross between Chinese dominos (known as pai gow) and the American game of seven-card poker. The game is played on a surface similar to a blackjack table using a 52-card deck plus one joker (the latter is not wild and can be used only as an ace or as a card to complete a straight, flush, straight flush, or royal flush). Up to six players make their bets, and the dealer deals seven cards face down to each player. Each player looks at his cards and then arranges or sets them into two traditional poker hands. The high hand is made up of five cards, and the low hand contains two cards. The highest two-card hand is five aces (four aces plus the joker). The casino dealer sets his hands according to fixed house rules. Once all hands are set, the dealer compares the players' hand rank with his hand. You win your bet if both your low hand and high hand have a higher poker rank than the dealer's low and high hands. If one hand is higher in rank and the other lower than the dealer's hands, this is a tie (or push), and you neither win nor lose your wager. If the dealer beats both of your hands, your bet is lost (you also lose if both hands are copy or identical in rank).

All winning bets are paid off at 1 to 1 odds or even money. However, every time you win, the casino collects a 5 percent commission (if you win a $5 bet, you are paid $5 but you must then give the dealer 25¢ as commission). You do not pay any commission if your bet ties or loses.

You must set your hands so that the five-card high hand is higher in rank than the two-card low hand; otherwise, you automatically lose the bet. It is a fairly simple rule to remember when you play.

If you get the gist of the game so far, you see it really isn't complicated. Although the dealer must set his hands by specific house rules, you can set your hands any way you want. Thus, there is an element of skill, because how you set your two hands often determines whether you win or lose the bet.

Is there an optimum way to set hands? Glad you asked, because in fact there is. Computer studies of the game have resulted in optimum ways to set hands. Space does not permit me to go over the entire strategy. The simplified basic playing strategy outlined below will get you started. The strategy is based on whether the initial seven cards dealt to you contain no pairs,   one   pair,   two   pairs,   etc.   (if   necessary,   put this strategy on an index card and take it with you when you play).

The casino's edge in pai gow poker with perfect basic playing strategy is about 2.5 percent. For more information about the game, and how it's possible to gain an edge over the casino, read *Optimal Strategy for Pai Gow Poker* by Stanford Wong.

Playing Strategy

The following is a simplified playing strategy for setting your hands in a game of pai gow poker.

◆ NO PAIRS. If your hand contains seven odd cards (no pairs), then play the second and third highest ranked cards in the low hand and the other cards in the high hand.

◆ ONE PAIR. Set the pair in the high hand and your next two highest ranked cards as low hand.

◆ TWO PAIR. If one of your pairs is aces, kings, or queens, split the pairs putting the high pair in your high hand and the low pair in your low hand. For all other pairs, play them as two pair in the high hand if you have a king or ace that you can use in the low hand. If you don't, then split the pairs with the high pair in the high hand and the low pair in the low hand.

◆ THREE PAIR. Play your highest ranking pair in the low hand.

◆ 3-OF-A-KIND. With three aces or kings, split them, playing the ace (or king) in your low hand and the pair in the high hand. For all other 3-of-a-kind, play them in the high hand.

◆ STRAIGHT & FLUSHES. Play them in the high hand.

◆ FULL HOUSE. Play the high pair as low hand, and the 3-of-a-kind in the high hand.

◆ 4-OF-A-KIND. Always split your four aces, kings, and queens. Play one pair in the low hand, the other in the high hand. With four Js through 7s, play them as 4-of-a-kind in the high hand only if you have at least a queen to use in low hand; otherwise, split the 4-of-a-kind (two in low and two in high). With four 2s through 6s, play them in your high hand.

♦ 5 ACES. Split the aces with one pair in the low hand and three aces in your high hand.

SIC BO

Sic bo is an ancient Chinese dice game. The object of the game is to select individual dice numbers or combinations of dice numbers that will appear on the three dice after they are shaken and exposed by the dealer.

There are 50 different betting options in sic bo. You can, for example, bet that the number 5 will show on at least one of the three dice. If it does, you win the posted payoff on the layout. Or you can wager that the number 5 will appear on two or all three dice. You can also wager that two different numbers, like 1 and 2, will show on two dice. Or you can wager that the total of the three dice will be a specific total (from 4 to 17). These are just several of the one die, two dice, three dice, and total sum betting options in sic bo.

The betting may seem complicated, but all these betting options are clearly marked on the layout. If you are not sure how to make a bet, simply ask the dealer.

The attraction of sic bo is the high payout for certain bets. Some pay $180 for a winning $1 bet! What is more important is the casino's edge on each bet. Some have an astronomical casino edge of 48 percent. Your best bet on the layout is to bet on either small (that's a bet that the total of three dice will be 4 through 9) or on big (bet that the three dice will total 11 through 17). These bets have a relatively low 2.8 percent casino edge.

For further information on sic bo, including a diagram of the layout and complete explanation of all the betting options, consult my book, *Reference Guide To Casino Gambling: How to Win*.

BACCARAT

All the casinos in Atlantic City offer baccarat and a lower stakes version called mini-baccarat. The rules for both games are the same.

Mini-baccarat is played on a table similar to a blackjack table. You have only three betting options. You can either wager on the bank hand, the player hand, or that a tie will occur. The tie bet has a very high casino edge and should not be made.

After players make their bets, the casino dealer deals two cards to two hands, called the bank and player hands. Whichever hand totals closest to 9 is the winner.

The value of the cards in baccarat is similar to blackjack with two exceptions. Picture cards count 0 and the ace counts only as 1. Also in baccarat, when the value of a hand exceeds a total of 9, you just subtract 10 to get an adjusted total (for example, a two-card hand of 5, 9 has a value of 4).

Initially, both the bank and the player hand are dealt two cards each. Fixed rules determine whether the hands get a third and final draw card. For example, the player hand must draw if the first two player hand cards total 0 through 5, and stand if they total 6 through 9. The bank hand third card draw rules are a little more complicated, but to play mini-baccarat it is not necessary to learn these rules, because the casino dealer determines whether either or both hands draw.

When you win a bet in mini-baccarat, you are paid at even odds. However, you must pay a 5 percent commission on all winning bank hand bets. The dealer keeps track of your commissions and you are expected to pay up when the cards are shuffled or when you decide to quit playing.

The reason for the commission on bank hand bets is that the third card playing rules favor the bank hand over the player hand. By charging the 5 percent commission on winning bank hand bets, the casino edge for both bets becomes nearly identical.

The regular game of baccarat is played on a much larger table in an area of the casino known as the baccarat pit. The rules are the same, except the players rotate dealing the cards and the stakes are higher (usually $25 minimums to $5,000 and up maximum bets).

The casino's edge in mini-baccarat is 1.17 percent for the bank hand and 1.36 percent for the player hand. Not a bad deal, but you can do even better. The Grand Casino recently lowered their commission on winning bank hand bets from 5 percent to 4 percent. No big deal, you say? That one percent drop in commission reduces the casino's edge by 43 percent from 1.17 percent to 0.67 percent. This is one of the best bets in the entire casino!

You can find more details about the game in my book *Winning Baccarat Strategies* or in the book, *Lyle Stuart on Baccarat*.

So there you have the basics of three popular Asian and European casino games. Next time you enter an Atlantic City casino, watch how these games are played and you will see they are not all that complicated. Compared to pouring money into slots or making most bets in roulette or craps, these games are not only fun to play, but they offer the smart player a better chance to walk away a winner.

♦ ♦ ♦

Baccarat Myths

I am often miffed when I walk through a casino and see thousands of players lined up in front of slot machines when maybe twenty yards or so away sits an empty mini-baccarat table with a dealer standing at attention, arms crossed, with a bored look. Doesn't anyone know that those slot machines are programmed to keep anywhere from 5 to 10 percent of all the money that is put into them whereas the house edge in mini-baccarat is only about one and one quarter percent? Oh, I know, what you are thinking. Baccarat is a complicated card game that is only played by high rollers. Really, now. Let's take a look at this and other baccarat myths.

"It's a complicated card game". This is absolutely false. In fact, it is probably as easy to play baccarat as it is to put coins in a slot. Really. You see, even though baccarat has rules, you can play the game without ever learning them. It's one of the few casino games where lack of knowledge regarding playing rules won't hurt you. In this game, the casino dealer is paid to know the rules, direct the players when to make bets, collect losing bets and pay off winners, and even deal the cards (in mini-baccarat). All you need do as a player is to decide whether you want to bet on the player hand or bank hand and just put your chips on the layout either on the player or bank and that is it! (There is a third bet you can make, a bet that the hands tie, but forget it because the casino's edge is out of sight).

"**Only high rollers play this game**". It's true that high rollers like this game because within a minute or less, they will know whether they won or lost (baccarat is a fast game relative to other casino games). But nowadays casinos have installed low stakes mini-baccarat tables on the main casino floor where the minimum bets are in line with the blackjack and crap tables (usually $5 and sometimes less). The only difference between baccarat played in what is affectionately known as the baccarat pits and mini-baccarat, is in the regular game the players take turns dealing the cards and in mini-baccarat the casino dealer deals. Of course the decor and dress in the baccarat pits is much more formal. In fact the strip casinos have lately been upgrading their baccarat pits to the tune of many millions of dollars all with the expectations of luring a high rolling player to their tables (I've seen many baccarat pits in my lifetime, but the new one at the Las Vegas Hilton, costing around $10 million, is a sight to behold).

"**The casino charges a commission on winning bets making it a bad deal**". Yes, the casino does charge a commission but only when you bet on the bank hand and it wins. Why do they do it? Because the playing rules for drawing cards for the player hand are different than the bank hand. And in the case of the bank hand, the rules are such that the player would actually have the edge over the casino. To change that situation and make the casino's edge about the same for both the bank and player hand bets, the casino charges a 5 percent commission on every winning bank hand bet. Even with the commission factored in, the casino's edge is about one and one quarter percent for both bets (in fact the casino's edge is 1.17% on bank hand and 1.36% on player hand).

If I still haven't convinced you to play baccarat, how about this. Some casinos in an effort to entice players to their baccarat tables, have reduced the commission from 5 to 4 percent. This lowers the casino's edge on the bank hand to 0.67%. Folks, it just doesn't get any better than this when it comes to gambling in a casino. And remember, unlike blackjack or craps where making a playing mistake could cost you dearly, the beauty of baccarat is that the casino's edge is fixed and you can't make it worse by making a stupid mistake. This is why baccarat is as close to a gamble as the casinos would care to have. In fact, a couple of high rolling baccarat players who gamble hundreds of thousands of dollars and get lucky and win will definitely hurt the casino's bottom line during that period.

Think about trying baccarat, especially mini-baccarat if you have a limited bankroll, the next time you are tempted to play the slots. Watch a game in progress to get the hang of it, then give it a go. If you want to know more about the playing rules, ask the dealer or pit boss for a free gaming guide which will explain the third card draw rules for the bank and player hand. With a little luck and that low casino edge, you'll have a much better chance of winning more over your lifetime than feeding coins into slot machines.

◆ ◆ ◆

The Grand Mistake

Sometimes casinos make mistakes in their listed payoffs for winning bets so that a player can actually have the edge over the casino. Smart casino players can turn these mistakes into money-making opportunities. This was the case at the Grand Casino in Biloxi where astute players cashed in on two bets in sic bo.

The casino game of sic bo is a dice game played with three dice. Players wager on different dice combinations. As most readers of this column know, casinos pay off winning bets at less than the true odds of winning the bet. This difference between the true odds and the casino payoff creates their edge and ensures them of a steady profit. Normally, every bet on the sic bo layout has listed payoffs at less than the true odds. However in the case of the sic bo layout at the Grand, two bets had listed payoffs at greater than true odds giving the player a tremendous 12.5% edge.

The two bets in question were on the 4 and 17. When you pick up three dice and roll them, you have 216 different ways (6x6x6) to roll the numbers 3 thru 18. In the case of the number 4, there are only three ways to roll it (1,1,2; 1,2,1; 2,1,1). Likewise the number 17 can only be rolled in three ways (6,6,5; 6,5,6; 5,6,6). Therefore the true odds of rolling a 4 or 17 with three dice are 213 to 3 or 71 to 1.

If the casino paid off a winning bet on the 4 or 17 at 71 to 1 odds, they would have no advantage. Normally they pay less (60 to 1). But in the case of these bets at the Grand, their layout showed an 80 to 1 payoff. Paying off winning bets at 80 to 1 with true odds of 71 to 1 creates the 12.5% player's edge.

I first learned about the 80 to 1 payoff from a local player who called me. I couldn't believe the casino would be paying off at these odds so I drove over to check it out. Sure enough, the payoff on the 4 and 17 were listed at 80 to 1. That was the good news. The bad news was that earlier that day the Grand had shut down the game. When I asked several floor supervisors why the game was closed I got a few "don't knows" and " I heard they were ordering a new layout". It turns out the latter was correct.

During the weeks that the table was open, several astute professional players had apparently cashed in. I learned this several days after my visit from a special issue of Stanford Wong's *Current Blackjack News* newsletter.   Wong is a professional   blackjack   player   and   well   respected author/publisher.   He is usually one of the first to report on money-making opportunities available to the player due to unusual playing rules or payoffs.   Wong calculated a player could have the expectation of winning $1500 per hour betting $100 on the 4 and 17.   It seems a host of professional sic bo players converged on the Grand and after management realized what was happening and the mistake that was made, shut down the game and ordered a new layout.

No question that this will go down in history as one of the biggest money-making opportunities for casino players. Unfortunately, for many of us (myself included) we weren't quick enough to take advantage of this situation.

◆ ◆ ◆

Suggested Reading

Blackjack

Blackjack Attack, by Donald Schlesinger. A collection of articles by one of the foremost experts in blackjack.

Professional Blackjack, by Stanford Wong. The bible for serious card counters.

Basic Blackjack, by Stanford Wong. Presents playing strategies for every conceivable variation in rules.

Blackjack: Take The Money and Run, by Henry J. Tamburin. Covers basic, intermediate, and advanced strategies.

Blackjack Wisdom, by Arnold Snyder. A collection of rantings by the game's most prolific blackjack writer.

Best Blackjack, by Frank Scoblete. Covers the basics to expert strategies in an easy-to-understand, straight forward language.

Craps

The Dice Doctor, by Sam Grafstein. Contains basic and more advanced playing techniques.

Beat the Craps Out of the Casinos, by Frank Scoblete. Contains several unique crap systems.

Craps: Take the Money and Run, by Henry J. Tamburin. Contains basics plus increased odds playing and betting system.

Roulette

All About Roulette, by John Gollehan. Contains the basics of the game.

Spin Roulette Gold, by Frank Scoblete. Clearly explains how to play and how it's possible to get the edge over the casinos.

Beating the Wheel, by Russell Barnhart. Explains techniques used by skillful players to win millions from biased roulette wheels.

Baccarat
Winning Baccarat Strategies, by Henry J. Tamburin and Richard Rahm. Contains basics plus effective card counting systems.

Pai Gow Poker
Optional Strategy for Pai Gow Poker, by Stanford Wong. Contains complete playing strategies for setting hands.

How To Play Pai Gow Poker, by George Allen. Excellent beginners book.

Video Poker
Winning Strategies for Video Poker, by Lenny Frome. Contains a complete optimum strategy for all different forms of video poker.

Video Poker, by Stanford Wong. Shows how it's possible to get the edge over the casino.

Victory at Video Poker, by Frank Scoblete. Basics and winning techniques.

10-7 Double Bonus, Deuces Wild, and 9-6 Jacks or Better Reports, by Dan Dancer. Basic, intermediate and advanced playing strategies.

Poker
The Basics of Poker, by J. Edward Allen. Good introduction to poker.

Slansky on Poker, by David Slansky. Good advice for hold'em, draw and tournament play.

Slot Machines
Break the One Armed Bandits, by Frank Scoblete. Explains basics plus where casinos place their loose and tight machines.

Slot Machine Mania, by Dwight and Louise Crevett. Informative book on everything you need to know to play slots.

Caribbean Stud Poker

Caribbean Stud Poker, by Stanley Ko. Contains basics plus thorough analysis of the game.

Let It Ride

Mastering the Game of Let It Ride, by Stanley Ko. Contains basics plus thorough analysis of the game.

Let It Ride, by Lenny Frome. Excellent beginner's introduction to the game with basic playing strategy.

Other Books

Smart Casino Gambling, by Olaf Vancura. An excellent guide book on casino gambling.

The Las Vegas Advisor Guide to Slot Clubs, by Jeffrey Compton. Explains how to get the most from slot clubs.

1998 American Casino Guide, by Steve Bourie. Comprehensive guide to casinos in all states.

Comp City – A Guide to Free Las Vegas Vacations, by Max Rubin. Unique book that explains how to get the most of comps from the casinos.

Casino Tournament Strategy, by Stanford Wong. Comprehensive tournament strategies.

The Frugal Gambler, by Jean Scott. Learn the "low-roller" techniques to casino comps.

Reference Guide to Casino Gambling – How To Win, by Henry J. Tamburin. Concise summary of the basic playing rules and winning tips for 25 popular casino games.

The Complete Idiots Guide to Gambling Like a Pro, by Stanford Wong and Susan Sector. Excellent how to play and win book for casino players.

INDEX